Euclid Public Library
631 E. 222nd Street
Euclid, Ohio 44123
216-261-5300

You Are Here

you are here

DISCOVERING THE MAGIC OF THE PRESENT MOMENT

Thich Nhat Hanh

TRANSLATED FROM THE FRENCH BY
Sherab Chödzin Kohn

EDITED BY Melvin McLeod

SHAMBHALA Boston & London 2009

SHAMBHALA PUBLICATIONS, INC.
Horticultural Hall
300 Massachusetts Avenue
Boston, Massachusetts 02115
www.shambhala.com

© 2001 Éditions Dangles, Saint-Jean-de-Braye (France)
and © 2001 by Unified Buddhist Church, Inc.
Originally published in French under the title *Toucher la vie*.
Published by arrangement with the Unified Buddhist Church, Inc.,
2496 Melru Lane, Escondido, CA 92026.

English translation © 2009 by Shambhala Publications, Inc.

All rights reserved. No part of this book may be reproduced
in any form or by any means, electronic or mechanical,
including photocopying, recording, or by any information
storage and retrieval system, without permission in writing
from the publisher.

9 8 7 6 5 4 3 2

Printed in the United States of America

♾ This edition is printed on acid-free paper that meets
the American National Standards Institute Z39.48 Standard.
♻ This book was printed on 30% postconsumer recycled paper.
For more information please visit www.shambhala.com.
Distributed in the United States by Random House, Inc.,
and in Canada by Random House of Canada Ltd

Designed by Lora Zorian

See page 144 for Library of Congress Cataloging-in-Publication Data

CONTENTS

EDITOR'S PREFACE

Breathing in, I know I am breathing in.

In this simple statement is the essence of Buddhist practice. You can build a satisfying and fruitful life on it. You can help yourself and others. You can experience the world as pure and joyful. You can even become enlightened.

Breathing out, I know I am breathing out.

In this book you will discover how far this simple act of mindfulness can take you. Guided by the great Buddhist teacher Thich Nhat Hanh, you will learn how Buddhist meditation will help you to harness your natural insight, wisdom, and compassion, and so transform your life and benefit those around you.

It is astounding—although Buddhist practitioners have been discovering and rediscovering this for 2,500 years—how far the journey goes that starts with a single breath. In this book, Thich Nhat Hanh shows us how the path of mindfulness and insight can wake us from the corpse-like state of self-absorption, heal our emotional wounds and improve our relationships with others, connect us with love and wonder to this beautiful universe in which we live, and, finally, help us escape the bonds of birth and death altogether. This is the journey that Thich Nhat Hanh will lay before you in this book. Taking it, of course, is up to you.

This is not a book of philosophy. It is not about Buddhism. This book *is* Buddhism, because Buddhism is a living lineage of transmission from teacher to student. Through this book you have the privilege of receiving direct teachings from one of the most important Buddhist masters of our time. I think of it as an extended guided meditation, a traditional form of teaching in which the master guides the students in real time along the path of wisdom. So I recommend you don't read this book so much as *listen* to it. You might even visualize yourself sitting in the audience as this great Zen teacher delivers his talks. As I read this book, I find myself very much in his presence.

Partway through the book there is instruction on how to listen to Buddhist teachings, but it might be helpful to summarize that now, before you start. As you read this book, keep an open, relaxed mind, alert but nonjudgmental, and follow Thich Nhat Hanh's instructions and contemplations as he offers them. Reading this book is not about following a logical argument (although the logic is impeccable); it is about experiencing a spiritual journey on the spot. If you take this approach, I guarantee you experiences of insight, wonder, and joy.

Thich Nhat Hanh is, after His Holiness the Dalai Lama, the best-known Buddhist teacher in the West. Although he is often seen as beyond such categories, he is undoubtedly the most widely known Zen teacher in the world. With the Dalai Lama and Pema Chödrön, he forms a troika of Buddhist teachers whose image and writings attract—and benefit—thousands if not millions of people. Like theirs, his fame is richly deserved.

Deeply trained in Buddhist philosophy and practice from a young age, Thich Nhat Hanh exhibits the mind of realization, the heart of love, and the skillful means of a great Buddhist teacher. Yet he is much more: a courageous warrior for peace, a statesman, a poet, a healer of wounds, a builder of communities, a scholar, a political theorist, and a prolific author. Among living Buddhist teachers, he is unparalleled in his varied interests, skills, and output.

There was a time when this versatility and engagement with the world was seen as a disadvantage. Early in his career in the West, he was seen by some traditionalists as watering down Buddhist teachings by adopting trendy Western political postures and New Age interpersonal techniques. This was before people saw that his community's principles were founded on the original rules of the Buddha's own *Sangha* (community), before they understood that political engagement is an inescapable reflection of Buddhist vows, before they read the many books that demonstrate the depth of both his scholarship and realization. This was before they realized that Thich Nhat Hanh's contributions to modern Buddhism were rooted not in the West but in his native Vietnam, where his principles were forged in the fire of war and shaped by the struggle for peace over a long and extraordinary lifetime.

Thich Nhat Hanh was born in central Vietnam in 1926 and became a Zen monk at the age of sixteen. In the early 1960s, Thich Nhat Hahn became an important figure in the Engaged Buddhist movement for peace and social justice in Vietnam. His vehicle was the School of Youth for Social Service (SYSS), a grass-roots relief organization he founded that rebuilt bombed villages, set up schools and medical centers, resettled homeless families, and organized agricultural cooperatives. Rallying some ten thousand student volunteers, the SYSS based its work on Buddhist principles of nonviolence and compassionate action. Despite government denunciation of his activity, he also founded a Buddhist university, a publishing house, and an influential peace activist magazine in Vietnam.

In 1966, Thich Nhat Hanh founded the Order of Interbeing, whose members were guided by what Thich

Nhat Hanh called the Fourteen Mindfulness Trainings. These apply basic Buddhist vows to social and political life and today guide the Engaged Buddhism movement that Thich Nhat Hanh founded in the West. One of the first six members of the Order of Interbeing was a young biology graduate who took the name Sister Chan Khong, who to this day is Thich Nhat Hanh's invaluable lieutenant. If you would like to know more about that period, I recommend Sister Chan Khong's autobiography *Learning True Love: Practicing Buddhism in a Time of War*. You will be filled with admiration for the courage, compassion, and dedication of Thich Nhat Hanh and his young followers.

Thich Nhat Hanh's work for peace and social justice earned the enmity of both sides in the Vietnamese conflict. He had studied at Princeton and Columbia in the early 1960s, and in 1966 he returned to the U.S. to lead a symposium at Cornell and continue his campaign for peace. The South Vietnamese government would not allow him to return home, and he remained an exile for the next thirty-nine years. In 1967, Martin Luther King Jr. nominated Thich Nhat Hanh for the Nobel Peace Prize, saying, "I do not personally know of anyone more worthy of [this prize] than this gentle monk from Vietnam. His ideas for peace, if applied, would build a monument to ecumenism, to world brotherhood, to humanity."

Today, Thich Nhat Hanh resides at Plum Village, the Buddhist center he established in France, and teaches worldwide. The years since his exile have been marked by continued work for social justice, a prodigious output of writings, the establishment of major practice centers and lay communities around the world, and teachings that have benefited millions. He dedicated himself to the plight of the Vietnamese refugees known as boat people, and he has worked with American veterans to heal the wounds of the Vietnam War. He has brought Israelis and Palestinians together to meditate and work for peace. In 2005, he returned to Vietnam for the first time since his exile and immediately began working to revive and modernize Buddhism in Vietnam, with special emphasis on the role of women.

Through his unique life experience, a combination of deep spiritual practice and frontline political activism, Thich Nhat Hanh has produced a body of written work that ranges from Buddhist scholarship to realistic, Buddhist-inspired commentary on the important issues of our time. It includes books of poetry; guided meditations; Zen teachings; addresses to police, prisoners, and congressmen; Buddhist philosophy; children's books; contemplations on love; and inspiring teachings for general readers.

As editor in chief of the *Shambhala Sun*, I had the honor of interviewing Thich Nhat Hanh several years ago. As I often do when I interview a Buddhist teacher, I asked him questions that were important to me personally, with the hope that they would also be important to readers. We talked about love and emptiness and life and death, the kinds of deep personal and philosophical issues he addresses in this book. This was not Thich Nhat Hanh the social and political theorist, nor Thich Nhat Hanh the scholar. This was Thich Nhat Hanh the deeply realized Buddhist teacher, speaking with compassion to a student who needed help. This is the Thich Nhat Hanh you will meet in this book, the Thich Nhat Hanh who may change the way you see your life. The wisdom in this book is simple, deep, and life-changing. This wisdom begins so simply: *Breathing in, I know I am breathing in.*

Melvin McLeod
Editor in chief
The Shambhala Sun
Buddhadharma: The Practitioner's Quarterly

You Are Here

ONE

Happiness and Peace Are Possible

Every twenty-four-hour day is a tremendous gift to us. So we all should learn to live in a way that makes joy and happiness possible. We can do this. I begin my day by making an offering of incense while following my breath. I think to myself that this day is a day to live fully, and I make the vow to live each moment of it in a way that is beautiful, solid, and free. This only takes me three or four minutes, but it gives me a great deal of pleasure. You can do the same thing when you wake up. Breathe in and tell yourself that a new day has been offered to you, and you have to be here to live it.

The way to maintain your presence in the here and

now is through mindfulness of the breath. There is no need to manipulate the breath. Breath is a natural thing, like air, like light; we should leave it as it is and not interfere with it. What we are doing is simply lighting up the lamp of awareness to illuminate our breathing. We generate the energy of mindfulness to illuminate everything that is happening in the present moment.

As you breathe in, you say can to yourself, "Breathing in, I know that I am breathing in." When you do this, the energy of mindfulness embraces your in-breath, just like sun light touching the leaves and branches of a tree. The light of mindfulness is content just to be there and embrace the breath, without doing it any violence, without intervening directly. As you breathe out, you can gently say, "Breathing out, I know that I am breathing out."

Buddhist practice is based on nonviolence and nondualism. You don't have to struggle with your breath. You don't have to struggle with your body, or with your hate, or with your anger. Treat your in-breath and out-breath tenderly, nonviolently, as you would treat a flower. Later you will be able to do the same thing with your physical body, treating it with gentleness, respect, nonviolence, and tenderness.

When you are dealing with pain, with a moment of irritation, or with a bout of anger, you can learn to treat them in the same way. Do not fight against pain; do not fight against irritation or jealousy. Embrace them with great tenderness, as though you were embracing a little baby. Your anger is yourself, and you should not be violent toward it. The same thing goes for all of your emotions.

So we begin with the breath. Be nonviolent with your breathing. Be tender with it. Respect it, and let it be as it is. You breathe in—there's an in breath, that's all. If the in-breath is short, let it be short. If the in-breath is long, let it be long. Do not intervene, or force either your in-breath or your out-breath. It's like looking at a flower: letting it be as it is, mindful of the fact that it is there, a kind of miracle. See the flower as it is. See the breath as it is. We let the flower be as it is, and we should not do violence to our breath either.

Then we move to the physical body. In practicing sitting and walking meditation, in practicing total relaxation, you embrace your physical body with the energy of mindfulness, with great tenderness and nonviolence. This is the practice of true love in relation to your body.

In Buddhist meditation, you do not turn yourself into a battlefield, with good fighting against evil. Both sides belong to you, the good and the evil. Evil can be transformed into good, and vice versa. They are completely organic things.

If you look deeply at a flower, at its freshness and its beauty, you will see that there is also compost in it, made of garbage. The gardener had the skill to transform this garbage into compost, and with this compost, he made a flower grow.

Flowers and garbage are both organic in nature. So looking deeply into the nature of a flower, you can see the presence of the compost and the garbage. The flower is also going to turn into garbage; but don't be afraid! You are a gardener, and you have in your hands the power to transform garbage into flowers, into fruit, into vegetables. You don't throw anything away, because you are not afraid of garbage. Your hands are capable of transforming it into flowers, or lettuce, or cucumbers.

The same thing is true of your happiness and your sorrow. Sorrow, fear, and depression are all a kind of garbage. These bits of garbage are part of real life, and we must look deeply into their nature. You can practice in order to turn these bits of garbage into flowers. It is not only your love that is organic; your hate is, too. So you should not throw anything out. All you have to do is learn how to transform your garbage into flowers.

In the practice of Buddhism, we see that all mental formations—such as compassion, love, fear, sorrow, and despair—are organic in nature. We don't need to be afraid of them, because transformation is possible. Just by having this deep insight into the organic nature of mental formations, you become a lot more solid, a lot calmer and more peaceful. With just a smile, and mindful breathing, you can start to transform them.

If you feel irritation or depression or despair, recognize their presence and practice this mantra: "Dear one, I am here for you." You should talk to your depression or your anger just as you would to a child. You embrace it tenderly with the energy of mindfulness and say, "Dear one, I know you are there, and I am going to take care of you," just as you would with your crying baby. There is no discrimination or dualism here, because compassion and love are you, but anger is too. All three are organic in nature, so you don't need to be afraid. You can transform them.

Let me repeat: In the practice of Buddhist meditation, we do not turn ourselves into a battlefield of good versus evil. The good must take care of the evil as a big brother takes care of his little brother, or as a big sister takes care of her little sister—with a great deal of tenderness, in a spirit of nonduality. Knowing that, there is a lot of peace in you already. The insight of nonduality will put a stop to the war in you. You have struggled in the past, and perhaps you are still struggling; but is it necessary? No. Struggle is useless. Stop struggling.

So I take care of my breath as if it were my tender little baby. I breathe in, and I let my in-breath proceed naturally. I rejoice in the fact that my breathing is there. Breathing in, I know that I am breathing in. Breathing out, I know that I am breathing out. I smile at my out-breath. This is how you can practice. You will get a great deal of joy out of it right away, and if you continue for a minute, you will see that your breathing is already different. After a minute of practicing breathing mindfully, without discrimination, the qualilty of your breathing improves. It becomes calmer, longer; and the gentleness and harmony generated by your breathing penetrates into your body and into your mental formations.

Try to breathe in this way when you experience joy. For example, when you are looking at a sunset and are in contact with the beauty of nature, practice mindful breathing. Touch deeply the beauty that is before you. I am breathing in—what happiness! I am breathing out—the sunset is lovely! Continue that way for a few minutes.

Getting in touch with the beauty of nature makes life much more beautiful, much more real, and the more mindful and concentrated you are, the more deeply the sunset will reveal itself to you. Your happiness is multiplied by ten, by twenty. Look at a leaf or a flower with mindfulness, listen to the song of a bird, and you will get much more deeply in touch with them. After a minute of this practice, your joy will increase; your breathing will become deeper and more gentle; and this gentleness and depth will influence your body.

Mindful breathing is a kind of bridge that brings the body and the mind together. If through mindfulness of the breath you generate harmony, depth, and calm, these will penetrate into your body and mind. In fact, whatever happens in the mind affects the body, and vice versa. If you generate peacefulness in your breathing, that peacefulness permeates your body and your state of mind. If you have practiced meditation, you have already discovered this. If you have been able to embrace your in-breath and your out-breath with tenderness, you know that they in turn embrace your body and your mind. Peace is contagious. Happiness is also contagious, because in the practice of meditation, the three elements of body, mind, and breath become one.

So as you breathe in, respect the in-breath. Light up the lamp of mindfulness so that it illuminates your in-breath. "Breathing in, I know that I am breathing in." It's simple. When the in-breath is short, you take note of the fact that it is short. That's all. You don't need to judge. Just note very simply: my in-breath is short and I know that it is short. Do not try to make it longer. Let it be short. And when your in-breath is long, you simply say to yourself, "My in-breath is long."

You respect your in-breath, your out-breath, your physical body, and your mental formations. The in-breath moves inward, the out-breath moves outward. In and out. It's child's play; but it provides a great deal of happiness. During the time you are doing it, there is no tension at all.

You are here for life; and if you are here for life, life will be here for you. It's simple.

The First Miracle of Mindfulness

PRESENCE

The first miracle brought about by mindfulness is your own presence, your real presence. With this energy dwelling in you, you become completely alive. When the energy of mindfulness is dwelling in you, Buddha is dwelling in you. The energy of mindfulness is the energy of Buddha. It is the equivalent of the Holy Spirit. Where the Holy Spirit is, there is also understanding, life, healing, and compassion. Where mindfulness is, true life, solidity, freedom, and healing also manifest. We all have the ability to generate this energy of mindfulness. Do walking meditation, breathe mindfully, drink your tea mindfully, and cultivate this energy that dwells in you, that illuminates you, and makes life possible.

The miracle of mindfulness is, first of all, that you are here. Being truly here is very important—being here for yourself, and for the one you love. How can you love if you are not here? A fundamental condition for love is your own presence. In order to love, you must be here. That is certain. Fortunately, being here is not a difficult thing to accomplish. It is enough to breathe and let go of thinking or planning. Just come back to yourself, concentrate on your breath, and smile. You are here, body and mind together. You are here, alive, completely alive. That is a miracle.

Some people live as though they are already dead. There are people moving around us who are consumed by their past, terrified of their future, and stuck in their anger and jealousy. They are not alive; they are just walking corpses. If you look around yourself with mindfulness, you will see people going around like zombies. Have a great deal of compassion for the people around you who are living like this. They do not know that life is accessible only in the here and now.

We must practice resurrection, and this is an everyday practice. With an in-breath, you bring your mind back to your body. In this way you become alive in the here and now. Joy, peace, and happiness are possible. You have an appointment with life, an appointment that is in the here and now.

It is necessary to come back to the present moment in order to touch life in a deep way. We all have the ability to walk in the Kingdom of God, to walk in the Pure Land of Buddha every day. You have all you need—legs, lungs, eyes, and mind—and with a little bit of practice, you can generate the energy of mindfulness within you, just like lighting a lamp. Once you have become truly alive, take a step and you will enter the Pure Land. You will enter into the Kingdom of God.

The Kingdom of God is not a mere notion. It is a reality

that can be touched in everyday life. The Kingdom of God is now or never, and we all have the ability to touch it—not only with our minds, but with our feet. The energy of mindfulness helps you in this. With one mindful step, you touch the Kingdom of God.

For me the Kingdom of God is where mindfulness exists, and it is a kingdom where there is compassion. The Kingdom of God, the Pure Land, is not a place where there is no suffering. Many people aspire to go to a place where pain and suffering do not exist, a place where there is only happiness. This is a rather dangerous idea, for compassion is not possible without pain and suffering. It is only when we enter into contact with suffering that understanding and compassion can be born. Without suffering, we do not have the opportunity to cultivate compassion and understanding; and without understanding, there can be no true love. So we should not imagine a place where there is no suffering, where there is only happiness. That would be a very naive idea.

We have spoken of the organic nature of things. Suffering is also organic. It is from garbage that we produce flowers; and similarly, it is from suffering that we produce understanding and compassion. I would not want to live in a place where there is no suffering, because in such a place I would not be able to cultivate understanding and compassion, which are the basis of my happiness. Happiness is a function of compassion. If you do not have compassion in your heart, you do not have any happiness.

The First Noble Truth of Buddhism is about recognizing the existence of suffering. We must get deeply in touch with suffering to develop understanding. One day, when you are looking deeply at the nature of suffering, you will see the way that leads to transformation, to healing, and to happiness; for it is precisely through touching suffering that we discover the Fourth Noble Truth, the path to healing.

The First Noble Truth is *dukkha,* suffering. The Fourth Noble Truth is *magga,* the path that transforms suffering into well-being. Things interexist; they interare. They are organic. There is no path to the cessation of suffering without suffering. The Buddha told us to embrace our suffering and to look at it deeply in order to understand its nature. We should not try to escape from our pain. We should look at it directly. Looking at suffering deeply, we will have deep insight into its nature, and the path of transformation and healing will present itself to us.

To me, the definition of hell is simple. It is a place where there is no understanding and no compassion. We have all been to hell. We are acquainted with hell's heat, and we know that hell is in need of compassion. If there is compassion, then hell ceases to be hell. You can generate this compassion yourself. If you can bring a little compassion to this place, a little bit of understanding, it ceases to be hell. You can be the bodhisattva who does this. Your practice consists in generating compassion and understanding and bringing them to hell. Hell is here, all around us. Hell is in us, like a seed. We need to cultivate the positive within us so we can generate the energy of understanding and compassion and transform hell. Hell is a matter of everyday life, like the Kingdom of God. The choice is yours.

We can touch the Kingdom of God in everyday life. There is no need to travel a great distance to touch the Kingdom of God, because it is not located in space or time. The Kingdom of God is in your heart. It is in every cell of your physical body. With a single mindful breath, a single insight that is deep enough, you can touch the Kingdom of God. When you are practicing mindful walking, that is exactly what you are doing—touching the Kingdom of God, walking in it mindfully, with compassion and understanding. The Kingdom of God becomes your kingdom.

Not a day goes by without my walking in the Pure Land. I see suffering, but I have compassion in me. This is something everybody can do. Don't underestimate yourself: you have the ability to wake up. You have the ability to be compassionate. You just need a little bit of practice to be able to touch the best that is in you. Enlightenment, mindfulness, understanding, and compassion are in you. Very simple practices—such as meditative walking, mindful breathing, or washing dishes mindfully—make it possible for you to leave hell and touch the positive seeds that are within you.

You can live in such a way that you are in the Kingdom of God every moment. This is not just a wish, and it is not a promise of some future happiness. This is a reality. An hour of mindfulness practice, even fifteen minutes, is already enough to prove to you that mindfulness is possible, that real life is possible. A beautiful sunset is something that exists; the song of a bird and the blue sky also exist. The paradise of forms and colors is always accessible.

Your eyes may be in good condition, but do you know it?

> Breathing in, I am mindful that I have eyes that are still in good condition.
> Breathing out, I smile to my eyes that are still in good condition.

In this practice, you touch your eyes with your mindfulness, and you have this simple insight: your eyes are in good shape, and they still exist. You only have to open them to make contact with the paradise of forms and colors, a true paradise.

Some people wait until they have lost their sight to appreciate their eyes. Blind people may hope that someone will help them to recover their sight so they can be in paradise once more. You, all you have to do is open your eyes, and the paradise of forms and colors is available to you. You are in paradise already, but you don't pay any attention to your eyes, even though they are a condition of happiness. You should recognize that your eyes are there for you, and they are so very precious. They are more precious than pearls.

Your heart is also there for you. Your heart works night and day in order to maintain your well-being. You take time to sleep and to rest, but your heart works nonstop to supply all the cells in your body with blood. Have you touched your heart with the energy of mindfulness?

> Breathing in, I am mindful that my heart is working night and day for me.
> Breathing out, I smile to my heart.

Your heart is like a flower. Is it still refusing to open? Is it still refusing to love? You must ask, "My heart, are you ready to open as flowers do?" You must ask it that.

When you touch and embrace your heart with the energy of mindfulness, you are already practicing love. When you touch your heart with your mindfulness, you see that you have not been very friendly with it. You have eaten and drunk in ways that put great stress on it. You have not done everything you could to keep it in good health, even though it is one of the basic conditions of your well-being.

The Buddha taught us to meditate on the body. He suggested that we lie on the ground and begin to breathe. Begin with breathing mindfully, while recognizing each part of your body. You can start with your brain. Then you turn your attention to your eyes, your ears, your nose, and your tongue, touching them with mindful awareness and smiling as you touch each one. You can send energy, tenderness, and gratitude to the various parts of your body. "My heart," you say, "I know that you are there for me, and I want to be there for you, too." In this way, you will stop drinking alcohol and you will stop smoking, because they are harmful to your heart. With mindfulness, these things will appear to you clearly.

What is love? Love is treating your heart with a great deal of tenderness, with understanding, love, and compassion. If you cannot treat your own heart this way, how can you treat your partner with understanding and love?

> My heart, I am here for you.
> My eyes, I am here for you.

You embrace your body with a great deal of tenderness. You know that your body needs you. You should be there for it and generate the energy of mindfulness to bring it harmony, peace, and relaxation. This is how you practice love meditation toward your body.

We all need to learn the techniques of deep relaxation, so we can deal with the stress of life's ups and downs. You should practice this technique of total relaxation every day, in your living room, with your partner, with your children. It is the way to love your body. It is the way to take care of your nervous system. This is very important. The basis of practice is to be here: "I am here for my breathing; I am here for my body; I am here for my troubles, for my depression, and for my suffering."

The Second Miracle of Mindfulness

THE OTHER

The first miracle of mindfulness is our true presence—being here, present, and totally alive. Then, if you are really here, something else will also be here: the presence of the other. You are here and the other is here. What is the other? It could be your heart; your eyes; your body; or your in-breath. The other is the sunset, the song of the birds. Or it could be your lover, your partner, your son, your daughter, or your friend.

The other is the Kingdom of God. If you are really here, solid and free, the Kingdom of God will also be here for you. The fundamental condition for recognizing the presence of the other is your own true presence. What is loving? It is recognizing the presence of the other with your love. This is not a theory; it is a practice. Whether the object of your love is your heart, your in-breath, your physical body, or your baby, whether it is your son, your daughter, or your partner, your declaration of love is always the same. It is: "Dear one, I am here for you."

Please try this practice. You can practice mindfulness of the breath for a minute or walk mindfully toward the person you love most in the world. Then you are truly here, truly present. You open your mouth and you utter the magic words of the mantra: "Dear one, I am really here for you." You embrace the presence of the other with the mindfulness that is within you.

If the other person is far away from you, you still can do this practice. The other will still be accessible to you. With this practice, there is no need to use the telephone or the fax machine. When you are truly present, the other is present, too; you are both included within the Kingdom of God.

When the other person realizes that his or her presence has been recognized and confirmed, he or she will blossom like a flower. To be loved is to be recognized as existing. Have you looked at others in this way? If you embrace them with the energy of mindfulness, with your true presence, this energy is completely nourishing. It is like water for a flower. A flower needs water to live, and the person you love needs your presence! Your presence is the most precious gift you can give him or her. "Dear one, I am here, really here, for you." All of us can practice this mantra. It really works.

Even one minute of walking meditation or mindful breathing will make it possible for you to be present and offer your true presence to your loved one. If you ignore the person you love, your loved one will not have the impression of being loved by you. "He is ignoring me, he is paying no attention to me, he doesn't love me," she will say to herself if you are not paying attention to her.

I knew a boy whose father said to him one day, "Tomorrow is your birthday. I want to buy you a present." The boy was at a loss. He knew that his father was very rich, that he could buy him anything, but the one thing the boy truly needed was his father's presence. His father spent all his time and energy staying rich, and as a result he had no time to give to his family. He could give them lots of money and lots of presents, but the thing that was most precious of all, he was unable to give his child. That is why the child was sad, and after a moment he said, "I don't want any present. It's you that I want."

Have you offered your presence to the person you love? Are you so busy that you cannot be there for that person? If you are a father or a mother or a partner, generate your own presence, because that is the most precious gift you can offer.

You know how to generate your own presence, so

now you can make a gift of it to the one you love. This is something very practical. It is easy to do, it costs nothing, and it can be done very quickly. You do not have to practice for years to see the results. One minute will do. So you should put what you have learned into practice right away.

The Third Miracle of Mindfulness
WORKING WITH POSITIVE AND NEGATIVE ELEMENTS

The third miracle of mindfulness involves maintaining your own presence and your mindfulness of the other. You are truly present and the other is truly present—you have to maintain both presences. You achieve this through the practice of mindful breathing or mindful walking. If the presence of the other is refreshing and healing to you, keep hold of this presence and nourish yourself with it. If there are negative things around you, you can always find something that is healthy, refreshing, and healing, and with your mindfulness you can recognize its presence in your life.

Perhaps you are in contact with too many negative elements. You have looked at, listened to, and touched things that are negative in nature, such as fear and despair. These negative forces are everywhere. When you turn on the television, for instance, you run the risk injesting harmful things, such as violence, despair, or fear. At that moment, you say to yourself with mindfulness, "I don't need these things. I already have suffering, violence, anger, and despair in me. I refuse to watch these programs. I am going to seek out things that are refreshing in nature, healing and helpful things. I will practice walking meditation; I will make contact with the blue sky, with spring, with the song of birds. I will play with my little girl, my little boy. I'll do those kinds of things."

You need to recognize that these kinds of positive elements exist and that you can benefit from their refreshing and helpful presence. If you are facing a sunset, a marvelous spectacle, give yourself a chance to be in touch with it. Give yourself five minutes, breathing deeply, and you will be truly there. Touch the beauty of nature in a deep way. That will do your body and mind a great deal of good. This is the third miracle of mindfulness—maintaining this precious presence in order to benefit from it.

If something negative comes to the surface, such as your despair and anger, or the despair and anger of your spouse, you need the energy of mindfulness to embrace it.

> Breathing in, I know that anger is there in me.
> Breathing out, I care for my anger.

This is like a mother hearing her baby cry out. She is in the kitchen, and she hears her baby wailing. She puts down whatever she has in her hands, goes into the baby's room, and picks it up in her arms. You can do exactly the same thing—embrace the pain that is coming to the surface.

> Breathing in, I know that you are there, my dear
> anger, my dear despair.
> I am there for you; I will take care of you.

You can do mindful walking or sitting meditation at the same time that you are embracing your pain, because this energy of mindfulness will help you hold your pain. Where does this energy come from? It comes from your daily practice.

That is why you should practice walking, washing the dishes, watering the vegetables, and any other activity with mindfulness. When you begin the practice, the seed of mindfulness is quite small, but if you cultivate it every day, it becomes much bigger and stronger. Every time you need this seed, touch it with mindful breathing. Then the energy of mindfulness will make its appearance, and you will be able to embrace the pain that is within you.

Even when you are driving your car, you can practice. Take advantage of that moment to cultivate mindfulness. In fact, you can practice quite well while you are driving a car. Breathe in and breathe out, and remain aware of everything that goes on inside you when, for example, you come to a red light. You look at the red light and you smile. The red light is not your enemy. It is a friend who is helping you come back to yourself.

About ten years ago when I was in Montreal, I noticed that the license plates on the cars had the phrase *Je me souviens,* "I remember." I turned to my friend who was driving the car, and I said, "Dear friend, I have a gift for you. Every time you're driving and you see the phrase *Je me souviens,* come back to yourself and practice mindful breathing with the thought, 'I remember to come back to the here and now.'" Since that day, my friends in Montreal practice mindfulness of the breath every time they see a license plate.

Je me souviens. A car license plate can be a bell of mindfulness. Even when you are driving your car, you can generate the energy of mindfulness. When you make breakfast, that is also a moment to cultivate mindfulness. Be mindful of the act of pouring hot water into a teapot. You breathe and you say, "I know that I am in the process of pouring hot water into the teapot," and you smile. It is not only in the meditation hall that we practice meditation.

So the third miracle of mindfulness is drawing benefit from the freshness of positive elements, and embracing the negative elements within and around you in order to pacify them. There are moments where your breathing is not harmonious. When you are frightened or angry, your breathing is of poor quality. You can notice this through mindfulness, smile at your breathing, and embrace it with the energy of mindfulness. "Breathing in, I know that I am breathing in. Breathing out, I know that I am breathing out."

You will need a minute to improve the quality of your breathing, and then fear and despair will be transformed, and anger also. Touch your breathing with mindfulness and your breathing will improve the state of your body and your mind. You can be sure of it.

TWO

The Heart of Practice

The heart of Buddhist practice is to generate our own presence in such a way that we can touch deeply the life that is here and available in every moment. We have to be here for ourselves; we have to be here for the people we love; we have to be here for life with all its wonders. The message of our Buddhist practice is simple and clear: "I am here for you."

In daily life, we are often lost in thought. We get lost in regrets about the past and fears about the future. We get lost in our plans, our anger, and our anxiety. At such moments, we cannot really be here for ourselves. We are not really here for life.

Practice makes it possible for us to be free—to rid ourselves of these obstacles and establish ourselves firmly in the present moment. Practice gives us methods we can use to help us live fully in the present. Practice makes it possible for us to say, "I am here for you."

The Buddha said, "The past no longer exists, and the future is not yet here." There is only a single moment in which we can truly be alive, and that is the present moment. Being present in the here and now is our practice.

The Five Elements

"I am here for you." It sounds very simple. But we should ask ourselves, what does "I" actually mean? The Buddha taught that "I" is a combination of the following five elements:

1. our form (physical body)
2. our feelings
3. our perceptions
4. our mental formations
5. our consciousness

These are called the five elements, or aggregates (*skandhas* in Sanskrit, literally "heaps"). They are the five elements that make up the personality, that make up our "I."

Suppose I peel an orange and divide it into five sections. This orange represents our personality. Physical form is the first section of the orange, followed by our feelings, our perceptions, our mental formations, and, finally, our consciousness.

We need to learn to see our physical form as a river. Our body is not a static thing—it changes all the time. It is very important to see our physical form as something impermanent, as a river that is constantly changing. Every cell in our body is a drop of water in that river. Birth and death are happening continuously, in every moment of our daily lives. We must live every moment with death and life present at the same time. Both death and life are happening at every instant in the river of our physical body. We should train ourselves in this vision of impermanence.

When we look deeply at the nature of things, we see that in fact everything is impermanent. Nothing exists as a permanent entity; everything changes. It is said that we cannot step into the same river twice. If we look for a single, permanent entity in a river, we will not find it. The same is true of our physical body. There is no such thing as a self, no absolute, permanent entity to be found in the element we call "body." In our ignorance we believe that there is a permanent entity in us, and our pain and suffering manifest on the basis of that ignorance. If we touch deeply the non-self nature in us, we can get out of that suffering.

The second element, the second section of the orange, is our feelings. Some feelings have their root in the physical form. For example, if you have a toothache, you have unpleasant feelings and you go to the dentist to get relief from the pain. Other feelings arise from perceptions.

Perceptions can be either accurate or inaccurate, and every time we have a false perception, suffering occurs.

We should train ourselves to see our feelings also as a river. In that river, each feeling is a drop of water. Feelings are born, take shape, last for a few moments, and then disappear. As with the physical form, birth and death of feelings occur in every moment.

In meditation, we look mindfully at this river of feelings. We contemplate their arising, their remaining, and their disappearance. We witness their impermanence. When we have an unpleasant feeling, we say to ourselves, "This feeling is in me, it will stay for a while, and then it will disappear because it is impermanent." Just by seeing the impermanence of feelings in this way we suffer a lot less. This is true for both the feelings that arise from physical form and those that arise from perceptions.

The third section of the orange is perception. Perception is a river too. It is impermanent. When I perceive something, I have an idea or an image of that thing. When I look at a person, a cloud, or a dog, I have an image of that person, that cloud, or that dog. That is the river of perceptions.

The Buddha said that our perceptions are very often false, and since error is there, suffering is there also. We must pay very close attention to this. We have to learn how to look at our perceptions without getting caught by them. We must always ask ourselves the question, "Is my perception accurate?" Just asking that question is a big help.

In most cases, our perceptions are inaccurate, and we suffer because we are too sure of them. Look at your perceptions and smile to them. Breathe, look deeply into their nature, and you will see that there are many errors in them. For example, that person you are thinking about has no desire to harm you, but you think that he does. It is important not to be a victim of your false perceptions. If you are the victim of your false perceptions, you will suffer a lot. You have to sit down and look at perceptions very calmly. You have to look into the deepest part of their nature in order to detect what is false about them.

The fourth section of the orange is the forty-nine mental formations, such as fear, hate, jealousy, love, understanding, compassion, hope, and so on. "Formation" is a slightly technical word we use to mean things, conditioned phenomena. There are physical formations and mental formations. A flower, for example, is a physical formation. Let us consider a flower. If we really look into its nature, we see sun, clouds, rain, minerals, soil, and the gardener. We see all the conditions that came together to manifest in a thing called flower. The flower is conditioned by what could be called the non-flower elements. The sun is a non-flower element, and the clouds as well. The non-flower elements have helped the flower to manifest.

When conditions are sufficient, something manifests. That is what we call a formation. The flower is a formation, and so are the cloud and the sun. I am a formation, and you are a formation.

Your anger and your hope are mental formations. In my tradition of Buddhism, we speak in terms of fifty-one mental formations. When I was a novice, I had to learn them by heart. The elements of feelings and perceptions are considered mental formations, but these two are considered to be so significant that they are treated as their own separate *skandhas.* That leaves another forty-nine. Our fear, compassion, anger, and mindfulness are among the forty-nine remaining mental formations.

Finally, there is the fifth element, consciousness. Consciousness is like the soil in which the seeds of the mental formations are preserved. Each of the fifty-one mental formations lies buried in the soil of consciousness in the form of a seed (*bija* in Sanskrit). When the conditions are sufficient, these seeds manifest as mental formations, such as perceptions, feelings, anger, compassion, and so on.

The seeds of negativity are always there, but very positive seeds also exist, such as the seeds of compassion, tolerance, and love. These seeds are all there in the soil, but without rain they cannot manifest. Our practice is to recognize and water the positive seeds. If you recognize the seed of compassion in yourself, you should make sure that it is watered several times every day.

So the practice consists of looking deeply into the ground of consciousness to identify the seeds that are there. These seeds were transmitted to us by our ancestors, including most recently our parents, and were planted during our youth. They are our genetic and spiritual heritage, and we need to be aware of them. Through the practice of deep looking, we can identify the positive seeds that we want to water every day, and train ourselves not to water the negative ones. This is called "selective watering." The Buddha recommended methods for doing this, and even a few days of this practice can bring about a transformation.

In summary, the "I" is made up of the body and mind (*namarupa* in Sanskrit). The physical form is body, and all the other elements are mind. When we look deeply into these five elements, we do not see any absolute, permanent identity. The five rivers are impermanent. If you practice in such a way that harmony is established in the realm of the five elements, then joy, peace, and happiness will be possible. Through breathing, through bringing your mind back to your body, through the method of deep looking, you will reestablish harmony and peace in the realm of the five elements. You will become a happy formation, pleasing to encounter, and you will be able to bring happiness to the living beings around you.

Unity of Body and Mind

"I am here" means doing what is necessary for the five elements of your personality to be fully established in the present moment. "I am here" is a practice, not a mere assertion. The verb "to be" here means to generate your own presence, your real presence. You must be here, with your body and mind united. In our daily life, we lose ourselves all the time. The body is here, but the mind is somewhere else—in the past, in the future, carried away by anger, jealousy, fear, and so on. The mind is not really present with the body. We are not really here.

To be truly here, we have to bring the body back to the mind and the mind back to the body. We have to bring about what is called the unity of body and mind. This is very important in Buddhist meditation. Often, the body and the mind go in different directions, and so we are not fully here. Therefore, we have to do what is necessary for them to come back together again. Buddhism teaches us methods for doing this, such as mindfulness of the breath.

The breath is like a bridge that links our body and mind. If you come back to your breathing, your body and your mind begin to come back together again. To breathe mindfully, you can say silently to yourself,

> Breathing in, I know I am breathing in.
> Breathing out, I know I am breathing out.

It only takes a few seconds of mindful breathing for your body and mind to begin to come back together again. It is very easy. A child can do it. You just concentrate on your in-breath and on your out-breath. You don't think about anything else. The past, the future, your worries, your anger, and your despair are not there anymore. Only one thing is there: your in-breath and your out-breath.

You have to deeply experience breathing in and breathing out. In a sitting position, you can really enjoy breathing in and breathing out. Go ahead and enjoy breathing for twenty minutes, just being here. You are here, and you have nothing to do except enjoy mindful breathing.

This practice can really be very pleasant. I'm breathing in, great! It's enjoyable, very pleasant. Imagine that you have a stuffy nose or that you have asthma. There is no air in your room, and you are suffering. Now, your nose is clear. You do not have asthma, and you have plenty of air. That's wonderful! You breathe out and you smile. This is a practice we can all do. Even children of five or six can begin training in mindfulness of the breath. In the summertime, lots of young people come to Plum Village, our monastery and practice center in France, and many of them practice mindfulness of the breath.

Descartes said, "I think, therefore I am." In light of the Buddha's teaching, you might say, "I think, therefore I am . . . not here." You are lost in your thinking, so you are really not here. For you to truly be here, thinking has to stop. As you are practicing mindfulness of the breath, the object of your attention is simply the breath. You stop thinking about the past, the future, your pain, your plans, and so forth, and you start to be really here, body and mind united.

When Nelson Mandela made his first visit to France, the press asked him what he would most like to do. He said, "Sit and do nothing. Ever since I got out of prison, I haven't had time to just sit down and do nothing."

Sitting on a cushion and doing nothing but breathing is something Nelson Mandela cannot do. You can do it for him. Be there with your breath. Use mindfulness of the breath to unite your body and mind. Establish yourself in the here and now so that you can touch life in a deep way, in this moment. Joy and happiness become real through mindfulness of the breath.

The Address of Life

You can practice "I am here" through mindful breathing and mindful walking. When you walk, you should be here. When you walk, it is not for the future; it is not in order to get somewhere. With each step you take, you arrive in the here and now. You can walk very slowly or you can walk fast, it's up to you, but take your steps mindfully. As you are walking, you can coordinate your steps with your breath. For slow walking meditation, one step is enough. One step: I breathe in. One step: I breathe out.

As you breathe in, you practice arriving. You have arrived. Your destination is the here and now. In daily life, you are in the habit of running because you think happiness is impossible in the present. This is a habit that was handed down to you by your ancestors, by your parents. Happiness does not seem possible to you in the here and now, so you look for it in the distant future. The practice consists of stopping that habit of running.

Remember the words of the Buddha, "The past no longer exists, and the future is not here yet." The only moment in which you can be truly alive is the present moment. The present moment is the destination, the point to arrive at. Every time you breathe in and take a step, you arrive: "Breathing in, I arrive. Breathing out, I arrive."

The address of the buddhas and the bodhisattvas is "here and now." That is the address of happiness, the address of life. The Buddha said, "Life is accessible only in the present moment." Life with all its wonders is accessible right now. So we train in coming back to the present moment.

When you are sitting on your meditation cushion, you are established in the present moment. At that moment, you touch life deeply. During walking meditation, you do the same thing. Each step brings you back to your true home, the home of your spiritual ancestors—the present moment. It is in the present moment that life, peace, joy, happiness, and well-being are possible.

We can also practice "I am here" when we are eating. We have to establish ourselves in the here and now in order to truly eat. All through the meal, we should really be here with the people at the table. As we chew our food, we should really be here with what we are eating. We can get deeply in touch with the food, which is a gift from the earth and sky.

I use *gathas,* practice poems, during meals. When I chew, I say, "I have arrived, I am home" Then happiness becomes a possibility. It is a great joy to be able to be here and have a meal with family or friends. We have nothing to do except to eat in such a way that peace and life become possible. Do not think about anything; do not do anything. Be truly here for the meal and for the others who are present.

There are two things that should be the objects of your attention when you are eating a meal. They are the food and the people around you. Touch these two deeply and live completely in the present moment so that you can experience peace, joy, and happiness. You can be extremely happy eating this way. You have to eat like a free person. Don't allow worries, thoughts, and plans to drag you away from the here and now. Having a meal is a very deep practice. You can eat in such a way that you touch the ultimate dimension of life.

Everything you are seeking, you should seek in the present moment. To put it in Christian terms, the Kingdom of God is in the present moment. We don't need to die in order to enter into the Kingdom of God; in fact, we have to be very much alive. With a mindful breath, with a step taken mindfully, we can enter the Kingdom of God. The Kingdom of God is now—or never.

Stopping and Deep Looking

Here is a practice poem you can learn by heart. It can also be sung:

> I have arrived, I am home,
> In the here and in the now.
> I am solid, I am free,
> In the ultimate I dwell.

You can use this poem during sitting meditation or during walking meditation. As you breathe in or take a step, you say, "I have arrived." Here and now. I am not running anymore. I have been running all my life, but now I am deciding to stop because I have learned that life is here. When you stop, happiness starts to be possible.

Stop! The street sign reminds you. Stop running, because life is here, in the present moment. We have to train in that. As you breathe out, you say: "I am home." I am already home, I don't have to run. I am at home, in my true home. The address of my true home is clear: life, here and now. Peace is something that becomes possible the moment you stop. Stopping is an essential aspect of Buddhist meditation.

If you look into Buddhist meditation, you will find that it has two aspects: first, stopping, and then, deep looking. When you achieve stopping, you become solid and concentrated. That allows you to practice looking deeply into what's here, and looking deeply into the nature of things brings insight. This understanding will liberate you from your suffering.

Stopping (*shamatha* in Sanskrit) and deep looking (*vipasyana*) are the elements of Buddhist meditation. Deep looking is possible once stopping has taken place. On the cushion, we must stop. During walking meditation, we must stop. Even when we are in the kitchen washing the dishes, we must wash the dishes in such a way that stopping is possible. Every moment of dishwashing should give you joy, peace, and happiness. If it doesn't, you are not washing dishes as a practitioner. The kitchen is a place of practice. The monks and nuns and laypeople of Plum Village always wash the dishes with mindfulness. When we wash dishes, it is not only to get the dishes clean. It is to live every minute of the washing. So wash each bowl and each plate in such a way that joy, peace, and happiness are possible. Imagine you are giving a bath to the baby Buddha. It is a sacred act.

"I have arrived, I am home." Through these two phrases, you can experience a lot of joy and happiness. When I walk over to the table to pick something up, I remain concentrated on my steps the whole way. In that way, peace and life are possible. When I walk, I don't hurry to arrive. Why? Because I arrive every moment. I have already arrived. We should train in that.

> I have arrived, I am home,
> In the here and in the now.
> I am solid, I am free,
> In the ultimate I dwell.

The fourth line of this little poem means the same thing as the first and second lines. You arrive in the here and now, the ultimate reality. This is truly the practice of stopping, and it is very important. We have been running all our lives, as well as in our previous lives, that is, in the form of our ancestors and our parents. Now we have to train ourselves in stopping. We can learn to stop and touch each moment of the day. When you walk mindfully, each step you take can heal and nourish you. It can put you deeply in touch with life, and life's refreshing and healing elements will be fully available to you. Get deeply in touch with the positive elements that are present in yourself and around you.

After walking for a few minutes with the words of this poem, you will see that you are much more solid. The past and the future can no longer grab you and pull you away from life. As a result, you are much more yourself. You have more sovereignty. Taking back your sovereignty is the practice. You are more solid and more free. The greater your freedom, the greater your happiness.

We are not talking about political freedom here. We are talking about freedom from distress, from attachment, from anger, from fear. You are free from all that. Your happiness comes from that freedom. Through the practice of stopping, you cultivate that solidity and freedom. Through the practice of stopping, you will achieve it.

"In the ultimate I dwell." There are two dimensions to reality. One is called the historical dimension, and the other is called the ultimate dimension. Suppose we are looking at the ocean. On the surface we see waves rising and falling. From the point of view of the waves, there is birth and death, high and low, rising and falling. There are distinctions between waves.

But each wave is made of a substance called water. It is a wave, but at the same time, it is water. Concepts such as birth and death, higher and lower, rising and falling apply only to the waves, not to the water itself. So the waves represent the historical dimension, and the water represents the ultimate dimension.

When we look deeply at our own nature, we can get in touch with its ultimate reality. This ultimate nature is free of birth, free of death, free from any notion such as high, low, this, that, and so forth. In Buddhism, we call this nirvana, or "suchness." Nirvana is the extinction of all concepts, such as existence, nonexistence, death, and birth.

You have this dimension called the ultimate within you. In fact, you are free from birth and from death, free from existence and from nonexistence. Your true nature is the nature of nirvana. If you are from the Christian tradition, you could say that this ultimate dimension is God. The Kingdom of God is free from birth and death, free from high and low, free from existence and nonexistence.

You know very well that the wave does not need to die in order to become water. It is water in the here and now. You think you are subject to birth and death, but if you touch your nature deeply, you will see that it is the nature of no-birth and no-death. This is something that can make your fear disappear, and true happiness can only exist when fear is no longer there.

Touching the ultimate dimension is very important. The wave can live the life of a wave, but it can also do better. It can live every moment of its life deeply touching its nature of no-birth and no-death, that is, its nature as water. If the wave realizes that it is water, its fear disappears. It enjoys its rising and falling much more. Rising is joyful, and falling is, too. There is no birth and there is no death. That is the highest level of the teaching.

Practicing with a Group

When we practice with a community, a *Sangha,* we should take advantage of the group energy. Everybody is breathing mindfully; everybody is walking mindfully. We can see the Sangha as a boat. We have bricks of suffering in us, and without a boat we are in danger of sinking in the river of suffering. If you throw a stone in the river, it will sink, but if you have a boat, you can transport tons of pebbles and stones. The same thing is true for your pain and suffering. If you know how to use the boat made of the energy generated by the Sangha, you will not be drowned in your suffering. Because you put your trust in the Sangha, you can have confidence. You can say to yourself, "I am surrounded by the Sangha. The Sangha is generating the energies of compassion and mindfulness. I have confidence in that."

The vow "I take refuge in the Sangha" is a practice, not a declaration of faith. We need to trust in the Sangha. It is made up of people who are practicing mindfulness, who generate the collective energy of mindfulness, every moment of the day. You should put your trust in that energy.

The energy of mindfulness is the energy of the Buddha, and it can be produced by anybody. Buddha is the ability to be mindful. Every time you take a step or breathe mindfully, you generate the energy of the Buddha. This protects you and heals you. But if you are a beginner, the energy you generate may not be strong enough to handle the suffering in you. You need to combine your energy with the energy of the group. In that way healing and transformation can take place very quickly.

So taking refuge in the Sangha is very important. Even if you still have a lot of suffering and pain in you, you need to place your trust in the Sangha. You should say, "Dear Sangha, I entrust all of my suffering and all my pain to you."

Learn to walk, learn to sit down and breathe, and let the Sangha help you. Cultivate solidity. You are somebody; you are something. You are a positive factor for your family, for society, for the world. You have to recover yourself, to be yourself. You have to become solid again. You can practice solidity in everyday life. Every step, every breath you take should help you become more solid. When you have solidity, freedom is there too.

Freedom is the basis of all happiness. Without freedom, there is no happiness. This means freedom from despair, freedom from resentment, freedom from jealousy and fear. Genuine practice is practice that helps you become freer and more solid. Every step you take, every breath you take, every minute of sitting meditation, and every bowl you wash should give you more solidity and freedom. If your practice does not bring you that, it is not genuine. It is not working. You should consult a brother or sister in the Sangha to change your way of practicing. The Sangha is always there to provide you with support.

"I am here" means that my body and mind come together in mindful breathing, in walking meditation. Our motto is: body and mind together. When you achieve that, your presence is genuine and you are truly alive. This genuine presence is the most beautiful gift you can offer the Sangha, and your brothers and sisters are doing their best to offer you their genuine presence as well.

So take advantage of their real presence and respond to them in kind. Offer them your presence and do not lose yourself anymore in the past, in the future, in worries or despair. Come back to yourself. Breathe properly, walk properly, touch the earth as a miracle, touch life as a miracle. Realize the unity of body and mind. In this way, you will offer something very precious: your genuine presence in the here and now.

THREE

Practicing Skillfully with Our Past

Our appointment with life takes place in the present moment. Does that mean we are against the past and the future?

If we look deeply at the present moment, we see the past and the future in it. The insight of interbeing also applies to time. We see that the present is made up of non-present elements, that is, of the past and the future. The past is always there, accessible. We can enter into deep contact with the past through the present. That is true for the future, too. Normally we say that the future is not here yet, but we can touch it right now by getting deeply in touch with the present moment. Because it is of an interbeing nature, the present cannot exist by itself. It interexists with the past and the future. It's like a flower that cannot exist by itself: it has to interexist with the sun and the earth. This is true for time, too. The present is made up of material called the past and the future, and the past and future are here in what we call the present.

The Buddha said that we should not be afraid of the past; but he did warn us not to lose ourselves in it, either. We should not feed our regret or pain over the past, and we should not get carried away by the past. We do need to study and understand the past, however, because by looking deeply into the past we learn a lot of things that can benefit the present and the future. The past is an object of our study, of our meditation, but the way to study it or meditate on it is by remaining anchored in the present moment.

We may say that the past is already dead, but ultimately the truth is deeper than that. The past is still here in the form of the present. We may think that there isn't anything we can do about the past anymore, but there is.

Perhaps we have done negative things in the past that we regret. It's a mistake to think that it is no longer possible to change the situation, that it is impossible to correct the past. We can correct the past. The past is here; and if we get deeply in touch with the present, we can touch the past as well, and transform it. Transforming the past is possible, thanks to meditation practice.

Suppose you said something not very nice to your mother while she was alive. You regret this, but she is no longer here for you to say to her, "Mom, I'm sorry. I feel terrible that I said such a thing." What can you do? You should get deeply in touch with the present and see that your mother is still alive in you. A mother lives on in her children; it is a scientific fact. We are a continuation of our mother, as a rose is a continuation of the rosebush. You are the continuation of your father and your mother. If your mother is no longer alive, you can touch her in yourself, because she exists in every cell of your body and consciousness.

We are the recipients of a genetic inheritance that comes from our mother, our father, and all of our ancestors. If you have a grandfather who lived to be ninety, this grandfather is still alive in you. If you are weak, if there are cells in you that are not functioning properly, you should call on that grandfather in yourself and say, "Grandfather, come help me." Your grandfather will manifest immediately; and you will know that your grandfather is not just a notion, he is a reality within you. Every one of your cells has your grandfather in it. This is a miracle that we can touch by practicing meditation.

So if in the past you said something to your mother that was not kind, today you can practice mindful breathing, call on your mother, and say to her, "I said these unkind words to you, and I promise not to do it again." At that moment you will see your mother smiling, because your mother is still there, in you, alive. Our ancestors are still alive in us, and we can call upon them anytime we like.

Your spiritual ancestors are also within you. Some of these ancestors are still quite young. Your brothers and your sisters in the Dharma, and the person who guided your first steps in practice, are your very young ancestors. Your teacher is your ancestor, and your teacher's teacher. The Buddha, Christ, the matriarchs and patriarchs are your spiritual ancestors, and they too exist in every cell of your body and your consciousness. So we don't need to travel through time or space to get in touch with our spiritual and genetic ancestors. If we dwell in the present moment, we can touch them in the here and now through mindful breathing and deep looking. It's amazing how we can do so many wonderful things while sitting on our meditation cushions.

When you see your mother smiling in every cell of your body, you will find that your regrets and complexes have been transformed. If you behaved badly in the past, if you have been destructive, you can do something about it. By touching the present deeply, you can transform the past. The wounds and injuries of the past are still there—they are within your reach. All you have to do is come back to the present moment, and you will recognize the wounds and injuries that you have caused in the past and those that other people have caused you.

You should be here for these wounds and injuries. You can say to them, "I am here for you," with your mindful breathing, your deep looking, and your determination not to do the same thing again. Then transformation is possible.

Beginning Anew

Beginning anew is a very serious practice in our Sangha. We are always practicing this. "Beginning anew" means being determined not to repeat the negative things we have done in the past. A new era begins when we commit ourselves to living in mindfulness. When we vow to ourselves, "I am determined not to behave as I did in the past," transformation occurs immediately.

To make a fresh start like this, we need to study the Five Mindfulness Trainings, a set of real and concrete methods for living our daily life in mindfulness. (These trainings are listed on page 135.) For instance, in the past we have eaten and drunk toxins unmindfully, bringing poisons into our bodies and our consciousness. Now we want to eat and drink with mindfulness. Practicing according to the Fifth Mindfulness Training is a highly effective method for cutting out food and drink that have bad effects on us and have caused us a lot of suffering.

Enlightenment, awakening, is possible for all of us. The Buddha was an enlightened person, and we all have this seed of enlightenment in us. When we get in touch with the Dharma, when we meet a Dharma brother or sister, enlightenment is happening already. Enlightenment is possible, maybe even today.

When we are enlightened, we know where to go and when to go there. If we see our path and know what direction to take, peace appears in us immediately. "I know where I am going": this is a very important realization. Then there is no more confusion.

A participant at one of our meditation retreats was an American who had fought in the Vietnam War. This former soldier had suffered a lot. One day during the war, he found out that many of his friends had been killed by guerillas. He was overcome by tremendous anger and wanted to avenge his friends, so he put explosives in some sandwiches and left them at the entrance to a village. Some children found these tasty-looking sandwiches, and they ate them. These children writhed and screamed in pain, and finally died, right before their parents' eyes. The young man went back to America, but that day continued to haunt him. He was unable to find peace, and he could not even stand being in a room with children. This went on for years.

When I met this man during the retreat, I told him that transformation was possible. "You killed five children, that's a reality," I said to him. "Each of these children is crying right now in every cell of your body. I know that. That's why you have had no peace. So you must continue to look more deeply. Children are dying right now, as we speak, because of war. They are dying for lack of food and medicine at this very moment, and you can do something to help those children. Why do you remain immobilized, dwelling on your guilt and pain? You are intelligent. You know that every day forty thousand children die of malnutrition. You can do something. You can save a child, two children, five children, every day. You must find the will to live a new way. You have to make a fresh start."

He made the decision to devote his life to helping children, and the moment he decided to live a new way, the wound in him began to heal. Beginning anew is a wonderful practice. We can all practice beginning anew. We can always start over. With the help of deep looking, we can illuminate the present and gain a better understanding of the past. The past is within our reach, and we can transform it through meditation.

It is also possible for us to touch the future in the present moment. The future is being made out of the present, so the best way to take care of the future is to take care of the present moment. This is logical and clear. Spending a lot of time speculating and worrying about the future is totally useless. We can only take care of our future by taking care of the present moment, because the future is made out of only one substance: the present. Only if you are anchored in the present can you prepare well for the future.

Although we should not lose ourselves in fear of the future, we can make plans for the future if we enter into the present moment to do it. This is what the Buddha recommends. Building a Sangha, reorganizing our family, reorganizing society—these are things we need to do. If we establish ourselves in the present moment, we understand that the past and the future are here, accessible in the present moment, and we can do these things. This is because time has the nature of interbeing.

Ruling the Kingdom of the Five Elements

Of course we have difficulties in our relationships, with our families, with society. But we also have difficulties in our relations with ourselves. Our tendency is to believe that while things are not going well outside of us, everything is just fine within ourselves. That's an idea we need to reexamine. We have conflicts and suffering inside. Sometimes we have the impression that we are unable to get in touch with ourselves; we feel alienated, and we always want to escape from ourselves. We hate ourselves and we have no confidence, so we just pretend that everything is fine with us. We should not think that the problem lies outside us. We have accumulations of suffering and conflict within us. We have a war going on inside.

The territory of the five elements (*skandhas*) is vast. It contains physical form, feelings, perceptions, mental formations, and consciousness. Every one of us is a king or a queen reigning over this territory, but not necessarily a responsible king or queen. In this territory there are a lot of conflicts, suffering, and darkness that we are always trying to run away from. According to the teaching of the Buddha, we have to go back to the territory of the five elements to set things right. We have to repair the mistakes of the past and create harmony among the five elements. This is the practice the Buddha recommends.

The gateway to this practice is through the breath. We can always go in through that door. In the beginning, we enter somewhat timidly, because we are constantly trying to run away from ourselves. We fear that if we come back to ourselves, all the suffering we have accumulated inside us, all the despair and conflict, will be right there waiting for us. Our universal tendency is to try to stay away from all this suffering, so we are always trying to escape from ourselves. Society offers us all kind of ways to do this: television, radio, novels, magazines, cars, telephones, and so on. We abandon our territory just like that, leaving it in a state of disorder and pain. We want to run away from it. Our culture and our civilization are characterized by this tendency toward escape.

But the Buddha advised us to do just the opposite. We have to come back to our territory so we can bring order and harmony to it. We must be responsible kings and queens. You are responsible for your territory, your Kingdom. Do not look for the Kingdom of God outside of it. We are afraid to face our inner pain, so we run away; but the Buddha says with great compassion, "Do not be afraid, my friend."

Armed with the energy of mindfulness, you can cradle your pain like a baby. You can say, "My pain, my distress, I am here. I am back, and I am going to take care of you."

We can come back to ourselves via mindfulness of the breath. That is the main door. The Buddha left us a precise instruction on this practice called the *Anapanasatisutta*. I have written a commentary on this sutra entitled *Breathe, You Are Alive*. It is accompanied by another sutra, the *Satipatanasutta*, on which I have commented in the book *Transformation and Healing: Sutra on the Four Establishments of Mindfulness*. This sutra describes the four basic practices of mindfulness: the contemplation of the body in the body, the contemplation of feelings in the feelings, the contemplation of the mind in the mind, and the contemplation of the objects of the mind in the objects of the mind. These are very deep and practical teachings that help you come back to yourself.

You should recognize your pain and cradle it like a baby. You should embrace your suffering in order to soothe it, calm it, and transform it. You can do that with the support of your brothers and sisters in the Sangha, which is a powerful instrument. Even the Buddha needed a Sangha. The Sangha holds and contains the Buddha and the Dharma. It is necessary to take refuge in the Sangha in order to deeply touch the Buddha and Dharma. Your physical body and feelings can be transformed by the practice community.

In walking meditation, you can harmonize the activities of your body, feelings, and perceptions. You take a step and you smile—walking like this brings you a sense of freshness and pleasure. In walking meditation, you cultivate the unity of body and mind, just as you do in sitting meditation.

Listening to a Dharma talk is also a practice. When you are hearing a teaching, you should sit in such a way that peace, relaxation, and ease are possible. Don't struggle. Just open yourself to allow the Dharma to penetrate you, the way rain penetrates soil. You should not use intellect to receive the Dharma. Instead, open your physical body to the Dharma so that it can penetrate every cell of your body. Intellect is not everything. The intellect can be like a sheet of plastic covering the earth, preventing the rain of Dharma from penetrating the ground of your being. The ground of your being contains lots of seeds, and it needs the rain to penetrate deeply into it. So do not use only the intellect. Do not compare and discriminate. Just open up to the Dharma rain, and let it penetrate you. Let the Dharma enter into you freely, and the positive seeds in you will be touched and have a chance to sprout. Give your intellect a vacation, and let your body and the depths of your consciousness receive the Dharma.

The practices of walking meditation and mindful breathing help us to generate the energy of mindfulness. This energy allows us to come back to ourselves, to recognize and care for our pain and despair. The Sangha can help us cultivate mindfulness. If you need a Dharma brother or sister to help, call on them. "My brother, my sister, I have a little energy of mindfulness, but not enough to care for my pain. I need you to help me." Your Dharma brother or your sister will help you—they can sit down and breathe deeply with you to provide you with support.

When you are with the Sangha, take advantage of its energy. Putting your trust in the Sangha is a positive thing, and when you have recovered a little bit of freshness and harmony, you will be able to do something to improve the quality of your relations with other people, too. But if you do not have this freshness in you, if you do not have understanding and compassion, then do not try to fix anything, because you will fail. In the past, you may have failed to improve a relationship that was causing you trouble. That's because you did not start from the right place. The right place to start is in your body, your feelings, and your perceptions. You must begin at the beginning, and give yourself some time to care for yourself, to cradle and care for your pain. Then you will begin to generate the energy of compassion and understanding.

Caring for Your Pain

Have you ever written yourself a letter? Have you ever had a talk with yourself? Have you spoken with the little girl or little boy who is there, still alive in you? This little girl or little boy is suffering and carrying a lot of wounds. Now it is time to come back and embrace her or him. Take the time to come back to the little girl or the little boy and say, "Dear one, I am here for you. I know you have a great deal of grief in you. I can feel there are wounds. I am sorry I abandoned you for such a long time. Thanks to mindfulness of the breath, I am back." This is an indispensable practice. Writing a letter like this creates genuine transformation.

"I am here for you." "For you" means first of all for ourselves. There is pain and suffering in us, and we have tried to get away from it. We have not practiced the true presence that allows us to soothe the suffering that is in us. We turn on the television, we pick up a novel, we make a phone call so we can escape from ourselves. We do this every day. We have to change this habit. We have to come back to ourselves so we can take care of the situation.

"I am here for you" really means "I am here for myself. I am here for my suffering, for my pain." You should look at your pain as though it were an abandoned baby. You should come back to yourself so that you can take care of this suffering baby. Your fear, your depression, your despair—that is the baby in you. It is yourself.

"My dear one, I have come back. I am here for you." Breathe in so that you generate the energy of mindfulness. With that energy, cradle your baby in your arms. "My suffering and my pain, I am here for you." This is the practice.

Developing true presence has two purposes. The first

is to make contact with everything that is beautiful, refreshing, and healing. We need that—we need the nourishment of a gorgeous sunset, a child's smile, the song of a bird, the company of a friend. All of these things are precious, and we should be there to touch them. This is the first thing that mindfulness lets us do.

The second thing that mindfulness does is allow us to come back to ourselves and embrace our pain. Most people are afraid to come back to themselves because that means having to face the pain inside of them. With the practice of mindfulness, the situation changes. We come back to our pain, but now we are well equipped with the energy of mindfulness that has been generated by mindful breathing and by meditation. We use that source of energy to recognize and embrace our pain.

This is very important. If you are unable to take care of yourself, how can you take care of anyone else? How can you take care of the person you love? When you are here for yourself, when you have reestablished some basic order and peace within yourself, then you can take care of the person you love. It could be your son, your daughter, your partner, or your friend. But if you are not able to be here for yourself, it will not be possible for you to be here for them. That's why you must come back to yourself.

There is a third thing that mindfulness does, which concerns our environment and society. If you are an environmental or peace activist, your work will be much more meaningful if you have peace, solidity, and freedom in yourself. Then you will serve society and the environment much more effectively.

"I am here for you" means that I bring myself back to the present moment so that I can reestablish order, harmony, peace, and joy in myself. After that, I am here to soothe suffering and to offer joy and happiness to someone else. Beyond that, I am here for the environment, for society, for all those who are suffering.

The Practice of Shining Light

The Dharma is here to suppport and enlighten you. At Plum Village, we have a practice called "shining light" in which we shine the light of our mindfulness on a situation. We shine light on the situation of our body, our feelings, perceptions, mental formations, and consciousness.

You must look deeply at the state of your territory of the five elements to see what should be done there and what should not be done. This is very important. If you live in a community, you can ask for the help of the Sangha. They have observed you—you are their brother or sister, after all—and they can tell you things about your physical body, your feelings, and your perceptions. You need their insights about you.

At least once a year in Plum Village, every monk kneels down before his brothers and asks them to shine light on him, meaning to tell him how they see him, to express themselves concerning his body, his feelings, his perceptions, his strengths and weaknesses. His brothers come together to provide him with the advice he needs. After having received the recommendations of his brothers, the monk prostrates deeply before them three times in thanks, and in the days that follow he tries to practice in the light of their recommendations.

This kind of love letter from your Sangha can help you see more clearly what you should and should not do; and you can do the same thing with your family, your parents, or your partner. You have a need for illumination and the other person does, too. So you can say to them, "My dear one, you must help me. I have my areas of strengths and weaknesses, and I want you to help me to see them more clearly. I have within me positive seeds, such as hope, understanding, compassion, and joy, and I try to water them every day. I would like you to recognize the presence of these seeds in me and to try to water them several times a day, too. That will be a pleasure for me, and if I blossom like a flower, that will be a pleasure for you, too.

"For my part, I promise you that I will do my best to recognize and water the positive seeds in you. You have very positive seeds in you, and I appreciate them a lot. Every time these seeds manifest, I am very happy, because at such times you are wonderful. You are so full of love and joy that I vow to water these seeds in you every day. I see as well that there are seeds of suffering in you, and I will make every effort not to water these. In that way I will not make you suffer, and I will not make myself suffer, either." That is the practice.

The other person might be your son, your daughter, or your partner. The two of you have to make a treaty. You have to have a sense of solidarity. Making such a treaty is a wonderful practice to make peace and happiness reign, in a community or in a family.

Deep Listening

There is a being called Avalokiteshvara. He is a bodhisattva, a remarkable being whose characteristic feature is his ability to listen. He practices deep, compassionate listening. The fourth training of mindfulness is this practice of compassionate listening.

Listening is an art we must cultivate. First you have to be able to listen to yourself before you can listen to someone else. You must not run away from yourself, but rather be very compassionate toward yourself. The practice of mindfulness will generate the compassion you need to cradle your own pain and suffering. Then, when you begin to understand and love yourself, you are ready to understand and love another person.

There is pain and suffering in the other person. They should have the chance to express it, and you can transform yourself into a bodhisattva in order to listen. Knowing how to listen requires patience and compassion, and fortunately, we can train ourselves in this. As I have said, you should not try anything before you feel sure that some freshness and compassion have arisen in you. Even a few days of practice will begin to establish compassion and understanding in your heart.

The practice of deep listening consists of keeping compassion alive in your heart the whole time that you are listening. You do not listen in order to judge, criticize, or evaluate. You listen for one reason alone: to offer the other person a chance to express him- or herself. That person is going to say things that irritate you. He or she might express disapproval of you, heap blame on you, say things that are false. You have to be ready to listen to anything. You have to say to yourself, "I'm listening to this person not to criticize or judge him. I'm listening to give him a chance to express himself, to provide him with some relief—that's all."

This is called compassionate listening. If you keep this intention alive in your heart, you will act as a bodhisattva. Practice mindfulness of the breath the whole time you are listening, and maintain this intention: "I am listening in order to make it possible for her to suffer less." If you can do that, then her negative words will not affect you. What she says might be wrong, it might be sarcastic, it might be intended to hurt you or to put you at fault; but as long as compassion is alive in you, you are immunized against suffering, and that is a wonderful thing.

This has always been true for me. When you are able to keep compassion alive in you, you do not suffer anymore. You see that the person you are listening to is suffering very much with his wrong perceptions, anger, and confusion, and that what he is saying is coming out of his pain. You yourself are not affected, because compassion continues to fill you. This compassion is the fruit of the understanding that comes from the practice of mindfulness and deep looking.

In Buddhism, it is said that love and compassion are made out of one substance, which is called understanding. If you understand, you can love. But if understanding is not there, it is impossible for you to accept and love someone. Why did he act that way? Why did he say those things? You should look deeply into these questions, and then you will see the causes of what you are dealing with. With this understanding, you stop blaming and criticizing. Your compassion is born of your understanding of the situation.

For instance, a girl who was sexually abused by her father has suffered a great deal. If she is very reactive later on, if she says things that are not completely normal, it is because she was abused during her childhood. If you can understand that, you will stop taking a critical view of her. "She has suffered so much," you will say. "I should help her, I should not be critical of her"; and compassion will fill you because understanding is there.

Deep looking directed toward the other person is what will bring you understanding. "Poor thing, he suffered so much as a child. He was mistreated by society, even by his own parents. He needs help." With this understanding, compassion begins to be aroused, and with this compassion alive in you, you can practice deep listening.

A good psychotherapist knows how to listen. In fact, all psychotherapists should regard Avalokiteshvara as a model. Avalokiteshvara is an excellent listener. He knows how to listen with a great deal of compassion. Some psychotherapists suffer so much themselves that they are unable to really listen to the suffering of the other person. Deep and compassionate listening is important training for psychotherapists and for all of us.

In order to help another person suffer less and to provide him or her with some relief, you have to behave like a bodhisattva of compassionate listening. With training in mindfulness, you will be able to do this. I am sure of this because I have confidence in the Buddha that is in you. The Buddha is always in you. You only need to bring him out, to provide him the opportunity to manifest. The Buddha appears in anyone who is enlightened, and the substance of enlightenment is mindfulness.

I remember once when a group of us was listening to a woman speak about her life. Most of us were monks. When the woman was a little girl, she had been abused by her father and her brother. Then she had been sold into the sex industry. You cannot imagine the depth of her pain. There were eight of us listening, but at a certain point she was unable to continue with her story. She sat there immobilized. Her pain had increased until it reached the point where it blocked her speech. We were all trying to be there for her with deep and compassionate breathing. We stayed like that for forty minutes. It was only after this long time that she was able to speak to us again. This shows that deep listening is possible. There are people who have suffered so much that they are not capable of expressing themselves, so we need to practice compassionate listening to give them the opportunity to do so.

We can all act like the Bodhisattva Avalokiteshvara and listen to other people. You actually could be the best psychotherapist for the person you love, because you know him better than anyone. To do that, you have to take a fresh look at your view of him and look deeply at the situation.

There is a lot that needs to be done in society—work against war, social injustice, and so on. But first we have to come back to our own territory and make sure that peace and harmony are reigning there. Until we do that, we cannot do anything for society. Let us begin immediately. What I recommend for all of us is to come back to ourselves and take care of the little boy or the little girl who inhabits the depths of our wounded souls. Then we will be calmer, more understanding and loving, and the environment will begin to change. Other people will benefit from our presence, and we will be able to influence them and our society.

FOUR

Healing Our Wounds and Pain

Here is a practice poem that you can use in everyday life, at any time, no matter where you are:

In; out.
Deep; slow.
Calm; ease.
Smile; release.

You can recite this no matter what you are doing—while you are driving your car, while you are watering your garden, while you are cooking, or before falling asleep—as well as during walking or sitting meditation.

"In; out." This phrase comes to us directly from the Buddha. What it means is, "Breathing in, I know that I am breathing in. Breathing out, I know that I am breathing out." That's the whole thing. It's simple recognition of what is happening: an in-breath, and then an out-breath.

Mindfulness is first of all the ability recognize what is happening in the present moment. It is simple recognition—without judgment or criticism, without suppression or attachment. I breathe in, and I am aware that the in-breath is here. I breathe out, and I am aware that the out-breath is here. There is no criticism or struggle. There is no effort either to reject anything or grab on to it.

Breathing in, breathing out.
The breath is flowing in.
The breath is flowing out.

You could also say, "in-breath, out-breath." Or even just: "in, out." It's very simple, yet you can regard this practice as recognition of everything that is happening in the present moment. "I'm breathing in; this is an in-breath. I'm breathing out; this is an out-breath."

During this time, all thoughts stop. The past, the future, your memories and plans—you drop everything. You are your in-breath, and as you become one with your in-breath, concentration occurs. This will give you a great deal of pleasure.

"Breathing in, I know that I am breathing in." Let me remind you again that this practice comes to us directly from the Buddha. You are free of any intention to judge, find fault, reject, or cling, and you maintain that freedom in relation to whatever is happening. When you get angry or depressed, it is the same. You simply recognize what is there—anger, depression, and so forth—without any sense of disapproval or rejection. If you recognize emotion as existing in the moment, you will not feel upset. There is no battle to win or lose—this is Buddhist meditation.

When you drink whiskey, learn to drink it with mindfulness. "Drinking whiskey, I know that it is whiskey I am drinking." This is the approach that I would recommend. I am not telling you to absolutely stop drinking. I propose that you drink your whiskey mindfully, and I am sure that if you drink this way for a few weeks, you will stop drinking alcohol. Drinking your whiskey mindfully, you will recognize what is taking place in you—in your body, in your liver, in your relationships, in the world, and so on. When your mindfulness becomes strong, you will just stop.

You do not have to struggle against a desire. There is no need for a battle within you. Mindfulness is something that embraces and includes things like desire, that recognizes them with great tenderness. Meditation is not about turning yourself into a battlefield where one side fights the other, because the basis of Buddhist meditation is nonduality. The habits of drinking alcohol or getting angry are also you, and therefore you must treat them with great tenderness and nonviolence. The essential point is not to create conflict, a fight, within yourself.

So we begin with simple recognition. Then, when the energy of mindfulness is strong and you have concentration, you can practice looking deeply into the nature of whatever is arising, and from that comes insight. Insight liberates you from all negative tendencies.

"Breathing in, I know that I am breathing in. Breathing out, I know that I am breathing out." This is very, very simple, yet it can give you a lot of pleasure. You cultivate concentration, and with that concentration, you touch life deeply. You are free at that moment.

Let me say a few words about adding the words "deep, slow" to this practice of breath awareness. "Deep" in this case does not mean we are trying to make our inhalation deeper. It simply means that after a few minutes of practicing "Breathing in, breathing out," you will notice that your breathing has become deeper and slower. As you breathe in, you notice that your in-breath has become longer. As you breathe out, you notice that your out-breath has become gentler. As a result, your practice becomes pleasurable, and this pleasure nourishes and transforms you.

The practice should be enjoyable and pleasant. The elements called joy and pleasure, *mudita* and *priti* in Sanskrit, are a very important part of meditation. If you are suffering during meditation, your practice is not correct. Practice should be enjoyable and pleasant. It should be full of joy.

So whether your practice is walking or sitting meditation, do it in such a way that joy and pleasure are possible. It is not supposed to be hard labor. And in your everyday life, just as you do not do violence to your breathing, do not do violence to your body, nor to your anger or depression. We need to treat them with a great deal of tenderness, because the essential thing in Buddhist meditation is not to create tension, conflict, or rift within yourself. The positive elements within you are you, and the negative elements within you are you also. It is necessary for the positive elements to acknowledge and cradle the negative elements, and if you do that, a transformation will take place. There is no need for the two to do battle.

Weathering Emotional Storms

Calm; ease.

If you find there is not enough peace in your emotions, your perceptions, or your feelings, you should practice calming them.

Breathing in, I calm my feelings.
Breathing out, I smile at my feelings.

When you are feeling yanked by strong emotions, you can practice like this. Assume a seated posture in which you can be solid; or you can lie down. As you breathe, bring your attention to your navel and to the movement of your abdomen. Your abdomen rises and falls—follow that movement. Do not think about anything. The object of your attention is solely the movement of your abdomen. "I breathe in, I breathe out. I breathe in, I breathe out."

A strong emotion is like a storm. If you look at a tree in a storm, the top of the tree seems fragile, like it might break at any moment. You are afraid the storm might uproot the tree. But if you turn your attention to the trunk of the tree, you realize that its roots are deeply anchored in the ground, and you see that the tree will be able to hold.

You too are a tree. During a storm of emotion, you should not stay at the level of the head or the heart, which are like the top of the tree. You have to leave the heart, the eye of the storm, and come back to the trunk of the tree. Your trunk is one centimeter below your navel. Focus there, paying attention only to the movement of your abdomen, and continue to breathe. Then you will survive the storm of strong emotion.

It is essential to understand that an emotion is merely something that arises, remains, and then goes away. A storm comes, it stays a while, and then it moves away. At the critical moment, remember that you are much more than your emotions. This is a simple thing that everybody knows, but you may need to be reminded of it: you are much more than your emotions. Many people have no idea how to face their emotions, and they suffer because of it. A lot of young people are like that, and they think the only way to put an end to their suffering is to kill themselves. Why do we have to die because of an emotion? We must practice this ourselves, and we must help young people to practice it.

You should not wait for emotion to appear before you begin practicing. Otherwise you will be carried away by the storm. You should train now, while the emotion is not there. So sit or lie down and practice mindfulness of the breath, using the movement of your abdomen as the object of your attention. I am positive that if you do this exercise for twenty days, ten minutes per day, then you will know how to practice whenever a strong emotion comes up. After ten or twenty minutes, the emotion will go away, and you will be saved from the storm.

The Practice of Letting Go

If there are things that are causing you to suffer, you have to know how to let go of them. Happiness can be attained by letting go, including letting go of your ideas about happiness. You imagine that certain conditions are necessary to your happiness, but deep looking will reveal to you that those notions are the very things standing in the way of happiness and are making you suffer.

One day the Buddha was sitting in the forest with some monks. They had just finished their lunch and were about to begin a Dharma discussion when a farmer approached them. The farmer said, "Venerable monks, did you see my cows come by? I have a dozen cows, and they all ran away. On top of that, I have five acres of sesame plants, and this year the insects ate them all up. I think I'm going to kill myself. I can't go on living like this."

The Buddha felt strong compassion toward the farmer. He said, "My friend, I'm sorry, we didn't see your cows come this way." When the farmer had gone, the Buddha turned to his monks and said, "My friends, do you know why you are happy? Because you have no cows to lose."

I would like to say the same thing to you. My friends, if you have some cows, you have to identify them. You think they are essential to your happiness, but if you practice looking deeply, you will understand that it is these very cows that have brought about your unhappiness. The secret of happiness is being able to let go of your cows. You should call your cows by their true names.

I assure you that when you have let your cows go, you will experience happiness, because the more freedom you have, the more happiness you have. The Buddha taught us that joy and pleasure are based on surrender, on letting go. "I am letting go" is a powerful practice. Are you able to let go of things? If not, your suffering will continue.

You must have the courage to practice letting go. You must develop a new habit—the habit of realizing freedom. You must identify your cows. You must regard them as bonds of slavery. You must learn, as the Buddha and his monks did, to set your cows free. It is the energy of mindfulness that helps you to identify your cows and call them by their true names.

Smile, release.

When you have an idea that is making you suffer, you should let go of it, even (or perhaps especially) if it is an idea about your own happiness. Every person and every nation has an idea of happiness. In some countries, people think that a particular ideology must be followed to bring happiness to the country and its people. They want everybody to approve of their idea of happiness, and they believe that those who are not in favor of it should be imprisoned or put in concentration camps. It is possible to maintain such thinking for fifty or sixty years, and in that time to create enormous tragedy, just because of this idea of happiness.

Perhaps you too are the prisoner of your own notion of happiness. There are thousands of paths that lead to happiness, but you have accepted only one. You have not considered other paths because you think that yours is the only one that leads to happiness. You have followed this path with all your might, and so the other paths, the thousands of others, have remained closed to you.

We should be free to experience the happiness that just comes to us without our having to seek it. If you are a free person, happiness can come over you just like that! Look at the moon. It travels in the sky completely free, and this freedom produces beauty and happiness. I am convinced that happiness is not possible unless it is based on freedom. If you are a free woman, if you are a free man, you will enjoy happiness. But if you are a slave, even if only the slave of an idea, happiness will be very difficult for you to achieve. That is why you should cultivate freedom, including freedom from your own concepts and ideas. Let go of your ideas, even if abandoning them is not easy.

Conflict and suffering are often caused by a person not wanting to surrender his concepts and ideas of things. In the relationship between a father and a son, for example, or between partners, this happens all the time. It is important to train yourself to let go of your ideas about things. Freedom is cultivated by this practice of letting go. If you look deeply, you may find that you are holding on to a concept that is causing you to suffer a great deal. Are you intelligent enough, are you free enough, to give up this idea?

I am becoming calm,
I am letting go.
Having let go, victory is mine.
I smile.
I am free.

The Dharma that the Buddha presented is radical. It contains radical measures for healing, for transforming the present situation. People become monks and nuns because they understand that freedom is very precious. The Buddha did not need a bank account or a house. In the time of the Buddha, the possessions of a monk or a nun were limited to the robes they wore and a bowl in which to collect alms. Freedom is very important. You should not sacrifice it for anything, because without freedom, there is no happiness.

How to Experience the Miracle of Life

Joy and happiness are born of concentration. When you are having a cup of tea, the value of that experience depends on your concentration. You have to drink the tea with 100 percent of your being. The true pleasure is experienced in the concentration. When you walk and you are 100 percent concentrated, the joy you get from the steps you are taking is much greater than the joy you would get without concentration. You have to invest 100 percent of your body and mind in the act of walking. Then you will experience that being alive and taking steps on this planet are miraculous things.

The Zen master Linji (also known as Rinzai) said, "The miracle is walking on the earth, not walking on water or fire. The real miracle is walking on this earth." Why should you not perform a miracle just by walking? A step taken with mindfulness can lead you to the Kingdom of God. This is possible. You can do it today. Life is too precious for us to lose ourselves in our ideas and concepts, in our anger and our despair. We must wake up to the marvelous reality of life. We must begin to live fully and truly, every moment of our daily lives.

When you are holding a cup of tea in your hand, do it while being 100 percent there. You know how to do this—one deep in-breath, one gentle out-breath, and the body and mind come together. You are truly there, absolutely alive, fully present! This only takes ten or fifteen seconds, and suddenly the tea reveals itself to you in all its splendor and wonder.

When I pick up a book or open a door, I want to invest myself in this act 100 percent. This is what I learned during my monastic training, when my teacher taught me how to offer a stick of incense. A stick of incense is very small and very light, yet the right way to hold it is with two hands. When offering the incense, you have to invest 100 percent of your being in your hands and in two of your fingers—the energy of mindfulness must be concentrated there. This may look like a ritual, but it is a really an act of concentrated awareness. I put my left hand on my right hand, and during this time, I concentrate 100 percent. The incense is an offering to the Buddha, but does the Buddha really need incense? This is actually an offering of peace, of joy, and of concentration.

During my first year of training at the temple, my teacher asked me to do something for him. I loved him so much that I became quite excited, and I rushed out to do it. I was in such a hurry that I did not leave the room as I should have. I did not close the door properly, with 100 percent of my being.

He called me back. "Novice," he said, "come here." I knew right away that something was wrong. He said only, "My son, you can do better." He did not have to teach me this a second time. The next time, I did walking meditation to the door, I opened the door mindfully, and I closed the door behind me perfectly.

Since that day, I have known how to close a door behind me. It must always be done with mindfulness—not for the sake of the Buddha, not for the teacher, but for myself. This is the way you create peace; this is the way you bring about freedom. You do it for your own happiness, and when you are happy, the people you relate with benefit from your presence and are happy too. A happy person is an important thing, because their happiness spreads all around them. You can be a happy person too and become a refuge for all the beings around you.

Concentration is the practice of happiness. There is no happiness without concentration. When you eat an orange, try to practice concentration. Eat it in such a way that pleasure, joy, and happiness are possible the whole time. You could call this orange meditation. You take an orange in the palm of your hand. You look at it and breathe in such a way that it reveals itself as the miracle it is. An orange is nothing less than a miracle. It is just like you—you are also a miracle of life. You are a manifest miracle.

If I am 100 percent there, the orange reveals itself to me 100 percent. As I concentrate on the orange, I get deep insight from it. I can see the sun and the rain that are in it. I can see the flowers of the orange tree. I can see the little sapling sprouting, and then the fruit growing. Then I begin mindfully to peel the fruit. Its presence—its color, its texture, its smell and taste—is a real miracle, and the happiness that comes to me from getting deeply in touch with it can become very, very great. A single orange is enough to give you a great deal of happiness when you are truly there, entirely alive, fully present, getting deeply in touch with one of the miracles of life that surrounds you.

Little by little you must train yourself for life, for happiness. You probably received a college degree that you spent years working for, and you thought that happiness would be possible after you got it. But that was not true, because after getting the degree and finding a job, you continued to suffer. You have to realize that happiness is not something you find at the end of the road. You have to understand that it is here, now. Mindfulness practice is not an evasion or an escape. It means entering vigorously into life—with the strength generated by the energy of mindfulness. Without this freedom and concentration, there is no happiness.

Engaged Buddhism means engagement not only in social action, but in daily life. The object of this practice is joy in everyday life, which is freedom. We should use our time with a great deal of intelligence, because time is not only money; it is much more precious than that. It is life. A day is twenty-four hours long: do you know how to manage it? You are intelligent and have lots of different talents, but do you know how to manage your days? You must invest yourself 100 percent in organizing the days that are given to you to live. You can do it.

With mindfulness practice, transforming your pain will become much easier. Joy and happiness will help you regain your balance and heal your pain.

You know that good blood circulation is necessary for the well-being of your body. The same is true for your psyche: you must live and practice in such a way that your consciousness benefits from good circulation. Bad circulation of psychological elements creates problems. Blocks of suffering, fear, jealousy, and distress are stuck in the depths of your consciousness. They cannot circulate, and they make you feel fear. That's why you have closed the door to your store consciousness, because you do not want these things to come to the surface. You are afraid of the pain in you, and so whenever there is a gap in your day, you fill it up with books or television so these blocks of suffering do not come up to the surface.

That is what most of us do. It's a policy of embargo. You do your best to forget what is inside you, and consume whatever is available to help you do that. In this way you create bad psychological circulation, and mental problems will soon appear. While you are sleeping, accumulations of suffering will reveal themselves to you in your dreams. They cry out for help, but you continue to practice suppression and repression. Depression, fear, and confusion may also manifest in the realm of the soma, in the body. You will have headaches and all kinds of other aches and pains, but your doctor will not be able to identify the source of the pain, because it is psychological in nature.

Buddhism teaches that the body and mind are two aspects of the same thing. There is no duality between the physical and the mental aspects. There is a Sanskrit expression, *namarupa*. *Nama* is our mental aspect, and *rupa* means form. We cannot make a distinction between the physical and the mental. Your hand is not just a physical formation; it is a mental formation at the same time. The cells of your body are not only physical; they are also mental. They are both at the same time.

Buddhism has found that reality sometimes manifests as psyche and sometimes as soma. "Psychosomatic" is the Western term; *namarupa* is the equivalent in Sanskrit. We should train ourselves to see "physical" things as not solely physical. In fact, "physical" and "mental" are no more than expressions.

The Humanist Manifesto, which was written in 1933, says that the mind-body duality should be rejected, including the idea of a soul that survives after death, because it also represents a duality. What do Buddhists say about this? Buddhism agrees that the mind-body duality should be rejected, but it does not say that the disintegration of the body represents a total negation. Buddhism helps us to see that neither the concept of permanence nor the concept of annihilation are applicable to reality.

Beyond Birth and Death

If we look deeply into the nature of reality, we will see that nothing is created or lost. As the Buddhist text called the *Prajnaparamita* says, there is neither birth nor death. Birth is a concept, death is too, and neither of these concepts is applicable to reality. We must make the effort to look into this truth deeply to confirm it for ourselves.

In our minds, we think that birth means we start from nothing and become something—that from nobody we become somebody. That is our definition of birth: from nothing comes existence, from nothing comes being. But that is absurd, because it is impossible for anything to come from nothing.

This piece of paper I am holding in my hand is something that exists right now. Can we establish a time and place of birth for this paper? That is very difficult to establish, impossible actually, because before it manifested as a piece of paper, it was already here in the form of a tree, of the sun, of a cloud. Without the sun, without the rain, the trees would not have lived, and there would have been no piece of paper. When I touch this piece of paper, I touch the sun. When I touch this piece of paper, I also touch the clouds. There is a cloud floating in this piece of paper. You do not have to be a poet to see it. If I were able to separate the cloud from the piece of paper, the paper would not exist anymore.

The true nature of this piece of paper is interbeing. Before taking the form of paper, it already existed in the form of sun, cloud, rain, and trees. In the same way, a human is not born from nothing. Birth is only a moment of continuation. It is a concept, not a reality. And if there is no birth, there is no death either.

The tradition of Zen Buddhism invites us to look deeply at reality with the help of koans, such as, "what was your face before the birth of your grandmother?" Where were you at that moment? You are invited to discover that. You embark on a journey in which you look deeply and see yourself back before your birth, even before the birth of your grandmother.

You did not come from nothing. That is impossible, just as it is impossible that the piece of paper came from nothing. It manifests in the present moment as a piece of paper, but in the past it manifested in other forms. You are asked to seek and discover your own face, your original face before the birth of your grandmother. This is a wonderful practice. If you follow this quest, you will have the opportunity to touch the nature of no-birth and of no-death, and fear will disappear. This is the language of Zen.

When the French scientist Antoine Lavoisier said, "Nothing is created and nothing is lost," he was saying exactly the same thing. The concept of death is that being turns into nonbeing. That is impossible. Can somebody become nobody? No. If we burn the piece of paper, we cannot reduce it to nothing. The paper will turn into heat, which will go out into the cosmos, and turn into smoke, which will join the clouds in the sky. Tomorrow a drop of rain will fall on your forehead, and you will make a new contact with the piece of paper. The ashes produced by the burning will rejoin the earth, and one day they will manifest as daisies. Do you have enough mindfulness to recognize the piece of paper in those daisies?

It is our idea of birth and death that takes away our peace and happiness in everyday life. And it is meditation that will rid us of the fear that is born from the idea of birth and death. This is the virtue of deep looking in meditation.

It helps you to see the heart of reality very deeply. To touch the nature of interbeing is to touch the very nature of no-death and no-birth.

The notion of death, of nothingness, is very dangerous. It makes people suffer a lot. In Buddhist teaching nothingness is only a concept, and it is never applicable to reality. The Buddha said, "When conditions are sufficient, the thing manifests, and when they are not sufficient, the thing remains hidden." There is neither birth nor death. There is only manifestation, appearance. Concepts like birth and death, being and nonbeing, are not applicable to reality. The wave on the water is free from birth and death. It is free from being and nonbeing. The wave is the wave.

The word *suchness* describes reality as it is. Concepts and ideas are incapable of expressing reality as it is. Nirvana, the ultimate reality, cannot be described, because it is free of all concepts and ideas. Nirvana is the extinction of all concepts. It is total freedom. Most of our suffering arises from our ideas and concepts. If you are able to free yourself from these concepts, anxiety and fear will disappear. Nirvana, the ultimate reality, or God, is of the nature of no-birth and no-death. It is total freedom. We need to touch this reality to leave behind the fear connected with the idea of birth and death.

We are afraid of nonbeing. "I am somebody, I am something," we feel. "Today I am, and I am afraid that one day I will no longer be." But it is impossible for being to become nonbeing. The Buddha said it in absolutely simple terms: "This is, because that is." This refers to the manifestation of phenomena on the basis of the law of interdependent origination. When conditions are sufficient, there is a manifestation. You could call that "being," but that would be inaccurate. In the same way, you could call the situation before manifestation arises "nonbeing," but that is equally incorrect. The situation is simply one of manifestation or non-manifestation.

Think for a moment about the space around you. It is filled with signals broadcast by radio and television stations. If you turn on a radio or a TV set, they will manifest in the form of images and sounds. Just because something is not visibly manifest, you cannot say that it is nonexistent, just so much nothing. In April at Plum Village, you do not see sunflowers. The hills are not covered with their blossoms, but you cannot say that there are no sunflowers. The sunflowers are hidden in the earth; they are just lacking one of the conditions for their manifestation, sunshine. It is false to say that the sunflowers do not exist.

So what is death? It is simply the cessation of manifestation, followed by other forms of manifestation. In wintertime, we do not see dragonflies or butterflies. So we think that everything is dead. But suddenly spring comes, and the dragonflies and butterflies manifest again. That which is currently not perceivable is not nonexistent. But we cannot say that it is existent either.

Existence and nonexistence are just concepts. There is only manifestation and non-manifestation, which depend on our perception. If you have perception that is deep enough, a deep insight into life, then you are free from all these concepts such as being and nonbeing, birth and death. This is the highest level of the Buddha's teaching. You are looking for relief for your pain; but the greatest relief that you can ever obtain comes from touching the nature of no-birth and no-death.

In Buddhism, we go beyond the concepts of creation and destruction, of birth and death. We also go beyond the concepts of self and non-self. We have seen, for example, that a flower cannot "be" by itself alone. The flower cannot be. It can only inter-be. We must go back to what the Buddha said—"This is, because that is"—and train ourselves to look at things in the light of interdependence. We can see the entire universe in a flower. We can see not only the entire universe, but also all our ancestors and our children in every cell of our own body.

Through Buddhist meditation you will experience the happiness of seeing and discovering wonderful things that will liberate you. We live in a time when everyone is too caught up in the preoccupations of everyday life, and we do not have enough time to live in suchness, with mindfulness. We do not take the time to touch things in depth, to discover the true nature of life. You are invited to use your intelligence, your time, and your resources to taste this timeless meditation that was handed down to us by our original teacher, the Buddha.

FIVE

Cultivating True Love

Four Mantras

In the springtime, thousands of different kinds of flowers bloom. Your heart can also bloom. You can let your heart open up to the world. Love is possible—do not be afraid of it. Love is indispensable to life, and if in the past you have suffered because of love, you can learn how to love again.

The practice of mindfulness will help you to love properly, in such a way that harmony, freedom, and joy are possible. The true declaration of love is, "Dear one, I am here for you," because the most precious gift you can give to your loved one is your true presence, with body and mind united in solidity and freedom.

You also have to learn how to speak all over again. When you speak with 100 percent of your being, your speech becomes mantra. In Buddhism, a mantra is a sacred formula that has the power to transform reality. You don't need to practice mantras in some foreign language like Sanskrit or Tibetan. You can practice in your own beautiful language: for if your body and mind are unified in mindfulness, then whatever you say becomes a mantra.

After you have practiced walking meditation or mindfulness of the breath for two or three minutes, you are here, really alive, truly present. You look at the person you love with a smile, and you say the first mantra: "Dear one, I am here for you." You know that if you are here, then your beloved is here also. Life, with all its miracles, is here, and among those miracles is the person before you, the one you love.

You can say this mantra a few times a day: "Dear one, I am here for you." And now that you have the ability to recognize the presence of this other person, you can practice a second mantra: "Dear one, I know that you are here, alive, and that makes me very happy." This mantra enables you to recognize the presence of the other person as something very precious, a miracle. It is the mantra of deep appreciation for his or her presence.

When people feel appreciated in this way—when they feel embraced by the mindful attention of another—then they will open and blossom like a flower. There is no doubt that you can make this happen through the energy of mindfulness. You can do it right away, even today, and you will see that the transformation it brings about is instantaneous. In order to love, we must be here, and then our presence will embrace the presence of the other person. Only then will they have the feeling of being loved. So you must recognize the presence of the other person with the energy of mindfulness, with the genuine presence of your body and mind in oneness.

If the person you love is suffering, you can say a third mantra: "Dear one, I know that you are suffering. That's why I am here for you." You are here, and you recognize the fact that your loved one is suffering. You don't need to make a big deal about it; you just generate your own presence and say this mantra. That's all. "Dear one, I know that you are suffering. That's why I am here for you." This is the essence of love—to be there for the one you love when she is suffering.

A mantra can be expressed not only through speech, but by the mind and body as a whole. The fact that you are there with the energy of your presence and understanding, and the fact that you recognize the presence of the other person and their suffering, will give them a great deal of relief. Some people suffer deeply but are completely ignored by others. They are alone and isolated, so cut off from the rest of the world that their suffering becomes overwhelming. You must go to them and open the door to their heart so they can see the love that is there.

Our bodies and minds are sustained by the cosmos. The clouds in the sky nourish us; the light of the sun nourishes us. The cosmos offers us vitality and love in every moment. Despite this fact, some people feel isolated and alienated from the world. As a bodhisattva, you can approach such a person, and with the miracle of the mantra you can open the door of his or her heart to the world and to the love that is always happening. "Dear one, I know that you are suffering a lot. I know this, and I am here for you, just as the trees are here for you and the flowers are here for you." The suffering is there, but something else is also there: the miracle of life. With this mantra, you will help them to realize this and open the door of their closed heart.

The fourth mantra is a bit more difficult to practice, but I will transmit it to you because one day you will need it. It is: "Dear one, I am suffering. I need your help." This fourth mantra is more difficult to practice because of the negative habit energy we call pride. When your suffering has been caused by the person you love the most in the world, the pain is very great. If someone else had said or done the same thing to you, you would suffer much less. But if the person who did it is the one who is dearest to you in the world, the suffering is really dreadful. You want to lock yourself away in a room and cry alone.

Now, when this person notices that something is wrong and tries to approach you about it, you might rebuff him or her. "Leave me alone," you say. "I don't need you." The other might say, "Dear one, it seems to me that you are suffering," but you do everything possible to prove you don't need them.

This is exactly the opposite of what you should do. You should practice mindfulness of the breath with your body and mind in union, and with this total presence, go to the other person and say the mantra: "Dear one, I am suffering. I need your help. I need you to explain to me why you did this thing to me."

If you are a real practitioner, please use this fourth mantra when you are in such a situation. You must not let pride come between you and your loved one. Many people suffer because of this obstacle called pride. You love someone, you need them, and so in these difficult moments, you should go and ask them for help.

In true love, there is no place for pride. I beg you to remember this. You share happiness and adversity with this person, so you must go to him or her and share the truth about your suffering. "Dear one, I am suffering too much. I want you to help me. Explain to me why you said that to me."

When you do that, the Buddha does it at the same time with you, because the Buddha is in you. All of us practice this mantra along with you—you have the support of the

Buddha, the Dharma, and the Sangha in uttering these words. These words will quickly transform the situation, so do not let things drag on for months or years. You should act decisively; the magic formulas have been transmitted to you for this purpose. Inscribe these four mantras in your heart, and use them. This is the practice of love, and its foundation is the energy of mindfulness.

False Perceptions

In my country, Vietnam, there is a famous story about a young couple who lived in the seventeenth century. The name of the young man was Truong, and his young wife came from a village called Nam Xuong. War broke out, and the young man was called up to serve in the army. His wife was pregnant, but he had to leave for the front all the same. They cried a great deal.

The young man stayed in the army for three years before he was allowed to come home. On the day of his return, his wife was very happy to see him. She went and stood at the entrance to the village with her little son, and when they met, they cried for joy. Then the young woman went to the market to get what she needed to make an offering to the family ancestor shrine. In our tradition in Vietnam, we make important events known to our ancestors, and in every household, even the humblest ones, the shrine to the ancestors occupies a place of honor. We clean the shrine every day, change the water in the flower vase, and offer a stick of incense. This is a daily practice to put us in touch with our roots.

In the West, too, we should live in such a way that we are connected to our ancestors. This is very important. Feelings of isolation and alienation come from a way of life that is too individualistic. We lose sight of the connection between others and ourselves, and between our ancestors and ourselves. That is why we must practice to keep in touch with those connections.

While the young woman in our story was at the market, the father tried to persuade his little boy to call him "Daddy." But the child refused, saying, "No, you are not my daddy. My daddy is another man who comes every evening. My mommy talks to him for a long time, and she cries with him. Every time my mommy sits down, he sits down also. And every time she lies down, he lies down too."

All of Truong's happiness evaporated on the spot. He became like a block of ice. (Perhaps your loved one sometimes becomes like a block of ice, too.) When the wife came back from the market, she sensed that something had happened. Her husband did not look at her or talk to her, so she prepared the offering silently in the kitchen. When she had finished, the husband placed the offering on the shrine, unrolled a mat, lit some incense, and touched the earth in front of his ancestors in order to announce to them his return. Then he rolled the mat back up without allowing his wife her turn to touch the earth. He thought she was unworthy to present herself at the shrine because she had cheated on him.

Instead of staying at home with his family to celebrate their reunion, he went to a bar and spent the whole day there trying to drown his sorrows. That is something many of us do. Because we do not know how to deal with our suffering, we resort to the use of drugs and alcohol.

For three days in a row, the young man did not come home until late at night. His suffering was too great. He never said a word to his wife or looked at her, and her suffering was also very great. By the fourth day, the pain was too much for her, and she threw herself into the river and drowned.

The young man, on hearing the news, went back to his house. That night he stayed with the child, and when it was dark he lit the gas lamp. Suddenly, the little boy began to shout, "There, there is my father," and he pointed to Truong's shadow on the wall. "Every night my daddy comes, and Mommy talks to him for hours and hours, and she cries a lot. Every time my mommy sits down, he sits down too."

The truth was suddenly all too clear. The man who had come every evening was actually the mother's shadow. The truth was that the young woman had waited faithfully for her husband. But one day the little boy came home and said, "Mommy, every other boy and girl has a father.

Where is my father?" So she pointed to her shadow on the wall and said, "That's your father. You can say, 'Good morning, Daddy,' and 'Good night, Daddy' to him." And she had talked to the shadow to convince the boy. Now the truth was out, but it was too late.

Wrong perceptions. All of us are only human, and we have wrong perceptions every day. Our spouse or partner is also subject to wrong perceptions, so we must help each other to see more clearly and more deeply.

We should not trust our perceptions too much—that is something the Buddha taught. "Are you sure of your perceptions?" he asked us. I urge you to write this phrase down on a card and put it up on the wall of your room: "Are you sure of your perceptions?" There is a river of perceptions in you. You should sit down on the bank of this river and contemplate your perceptions.

Most of our perceptions, the Buddha said, are false. Are you sure of your perceptions? This question is addressed to you. It is a bell of mindfulness. You have made mistakes; the other person has also made mistakes; and you need each other to let go of your false perceptions. Suffering and pain are born from wrong perceptions. Some people carry wrong perceptions with them to their deaths, and that causes a lot of suffering and misfortune.

When the people of the village heard about the mother's suicide, they organized her funeral and built a temple to her, which is still standing on the bank of the river where she died. It is called the temple of the Nam Xuong Lady. Everybody in Vietnam knows her story, but I do not know how many have learned the lesson of this tragedy. If that couple had been familiar with the fourth mantra, they could have avoided it. The young husband could simply have said to his wife, "I am suffering deeply, and I need you to help me. I need you to tell me who that person was who used to come here every evening, with whom you had long talks, and who sat down every time you sat down." It would have been a very simple thing, quickly done. And yet he behaved otherwise.

In the Eightfold Path of right practice that was presented by the Buddha, we find both right action and right speech. Saying this mantra is both right action and right speech. If the husband had said the mantra, his wife would have had a chance to express herself, and they would have avoided the tragedy. The young woman also should have come to him and said the mantra: "My good husband, I am suffering deeply, and I need you to help me. Why, since I came home from the market, have you not spoken to me or looked at me?" It only would have taken half a minute to perform the right action. And the tragedy would have been avoided.

My friends, I wish with all my heart that you do not make the same mistake. The next time you are suffering, if this suffering was caused by the person you love most in the world, have recourse to right action and say the fourth mantra: "Dear one, I am suffering deeply. I need you to help me to get out of this suffering. I need you to explain this to me." This is the language of true love.

SIX

The Essence of the Buddha's Teaching

There are three marks that prove whether something is an authentic Buddhist teaching. If you are not sure that a teaching you have received is authentic, you should refer to these marks. They are called the three Dharma Seals.

1. Impermanence

First of all, every authentic Dharma teaching bears the mark of impermanence. Any teaching that does not convey the truth of impermanence is not authentically Buddhist.

When you look at the nature of things with concentration, you discover that they are all impermanent. Everything is constantly changing. Nothing has a permanent identity. This impermanence is not a negative thing.

If things were not impermanent, growth would be impossible, and manifestation would be impossible. If things were not impermanent, you could not have children, and your children would never grow up. When you sow corn seeds, they would never be able to grow. They would remain corn seeds forever.

Impermanence is the very heart of life. It makes life possible. Reject impermanence, and you reject life. You should not complain about impermanence. Instead, you should shout, "Long live impermanence!" It is because of impermanence that everything is possible. Our hope lies in impermanence. Take the example of a dictatorship. How would it be if that were permanent? Impermanence is what puts an end to dictatorship. It's what puts an end to hatred and suffering, as well. We need impermanence to transform them. So do not be afraid of impermanence.

We must train ourselves to see things as they are. Take a river. There is no permanent identity in a river. We call it the Mississippi, the Rhine, or the Seine, and we think it is a single, permanent entity. But everybody knows you cannot step into the same river twice. A river is in a constant process of transformation, and so are we. We are made of elements called form, feelings, perceptions, mental formations, and consciousness. These things are aspects of manifestation, and you should look deeply into their nature. A feeling or a perception is very real, but you cannot find anything permanent in it. You cannot detect a permanent presence in anything whatsoever. You will never find anywhere a self, or a soul, that lasts.

In popular Buddhism, mention is sometimes made of a soul that outlasts physical death and lives another life. But that is not really what the Buddha taught. Does the soul exist according to Buddhism? If you believe that the soul consists of feelings, perceptions, mental formations, and consciousness, then yes, it exists—but impermanently. All these things are impermanent, just like the body. The continuation of life after death is possible, yet nothing is permanent. There is only continuation, only manifestation, because birth and death are just ideas. Being and nonbeing are just concepts. Reality is free from all these ideas and concepts.

If nothing is permanent, someone once asked me, what is the karma that we experience in future lives based on? But is it necessary to have a permanent entity for life to continue? Look at the example of a corn seed sown in moist ground. As a result of the right conditions—water, earth, warmth—the seed sprouts and produces little leaves. That corn seed is a very beautiful thing, thanks to impermanence. "If only that seed wouldn't die!" you might feel. But if the seed did not die, the plant could not grow.

We have to see that what is happening is not the death of the seed, but the transformation of the seed into a plant. Can we detect a permanent entity in either the seed or the plant? No. A permanent entity is not necessary to make life possible. With time, the little plant will become a big plant, which will produce flowers and then ears of corn. Is a self needed to make it possible for the corn plant to grow and then produce flowers and fruit? No, and the same is true for us.

We have no need of a separate self or a separate existence. In fact, nothing can exist by itself. We must inter-be with all things. Look at a flower. It cannot exist by itself. It can only inter-be with the whole cosmos. And that is true for you, too.

Getting rid of the concept of self is the work of all meditators, because suffering is born from this concept. If you detect in a teaching any allusion to the presence of a permanent entity or self, then you will know that this teaching is not authentically Buddhist, even if it makes use of Buddhist terminology. An authentic Buddhist teaching must bear the mark of impermanence.

2. Non-Self

Deep insight into the truth of impermanence leads to the insight of non-self. Non-self (*anatman*) is the second mark of an authentic Buddhist teaching.

Non-self is something miraculous. When we look deeply at a flower, we see all the non-flower elements there, such as earth, sun, minerals, the gardener, and so on. If we look deeply enough, we will see that the whole cosmos has come together to manifest as this miracle. The flower is full of all the elements of the cosmos—time, space, the sun, rain, even your consciousness—everything. But the flower is empty of one thing. It is full of all things, but it is empty of one thing: a separate existence. It is empty of any separate entity called self.

We are like the flower. Every one of us is a miraculous flower in the garden of humanity. If you look deeply into yourself, you will see that you possess everything. As the poet Walt Whitman said, "I am large, I contain multitudes." The one contains all—that is the insight of Buddhism. If you practice deep looking, you will discover this truth, the mystery of interbeing: the one contains all.

What you are looking for is already in you. You might have an inferiority complex and think that all you have in you is suffering. That is not true. You must get beyond the thought, "I am nothing. I am made up only of suffering. I should go look for a teacher who can save me." You must definitely get beyond this thought. You already are everything you are seeking. Do not try to become something else.

The flower does not try to become the sun; it already is the sun. It does not try to become a tulip; it already contains the qualities of a tulip within it. When you achieve this insight, you stop suffering. We suffer because we want to deny ourselves. We want to become something else, and so we never stop running.

There is a Buddhist teaching that might seem strange

to you. This is the teaching of aimlessness (*apranihita* in Sanskrit). Aimlessness is a form of concentration, one of three practices of deep looking recommended by the Buddha. The other two are concentration on the absence of distinguishing signs (*alakshana*) and concentration on emptiness (*sunyata*). So emptiness, signlessness, and aimlessness—*sunyata*, *alakshana*, and *apranihita*—are known as the three concentrations, the three meditations. They are the basis of Buddhist meditation, and all Buddhist schools transmit this teaching on the three concentrations, the three Dharma Seals.

Aimlessness means not setting an object or goal in front of you and running after it. That is exactly what everybody does. We want this, we want that, and as long as we haven't got it, we think happiness will be impossible. We must bring about a revolution in our thinking: we must stop. We must do as the flower does. The flower is aware of the fact that it contains everything within it, the whole cosmos, and it does not try to become something else. The wave is already water. Does the wave have to go looking for water? No. It is the same for you. You have God within you, so you do not have to look for God.

André Gide said something like the following: "Happiness is God, and God is accessible twenty-four hours a day." Water is accessible to the wave twenty-four hours a day. Peace, solidity, and the light of God inhabit you and are accessible at any time. And yet you keep running. Year after year, lifetime after lifetime, you keep looking. You must come back to yourself to touch the ground of your being, the ultimate dimension of reality, nirvana.

Nirvana has the nature of no-birth and no-death, and so there is no need at all for you to be afraid. Have you ever played with a kaleidoscope? Just a small movement is enough to make something miraculous appear. A tableau of colors and forms is presented to you, a manifestation. You keep this view for a few seconds, then you turn the kaleidoscope and another manifestation appears. Should we cry every time one of these manifestations comes to an end? A flower manifests, then disappears, then manifests, then disappears—thousands upon thousands of times. If you look deeply at things, you will see this reality. We manifest, then disappear. It is a game of hide and seek.

The person you have lost is still here. If you have the Buddha eye, you will see him. He is in the dimension known as the ultimate—he is smiling at you, and you should return his smile. Birth and death are only ideas, and reality is free from all concepts. Ideas have caused you to suffer, so be suspicious of your ideas.

You are a manifestation. You are impermanent. Yet you are full of all the elements of the cosmos. You are a miracle. You are already what you are seeking to become. When you have this insight, you can stop. Stopping is peace. Stopping is happiness. Buddhist meditation consists of stopping and looking deeply, *samatha* and *vipasyana*. Deep looking helps you to stop, and stopping helps you to look deeply. Those two help each other. In order to look, you have to stop, and when you are looking deeply, you are stoping.

3. Nirvana

The third mark of an authentic Buddhist teaching is nirvana. Nirvana is the basis of everything, as water is the basis of any wave. If the wave meditates, if it takes a moment to look at its own nature, it recognizes that it contains all the other waves. It is like the flower—it contains the whole cosmos.

Look into yourself and you will see that you are not a separate entity. Your ancestors are present in you, as well as your children and grandchildren. Not only is the past here in the form of the present; the future is here, too. When you look at orange blossoms, you do not see oranges. But if you are a meditator, you see the oranges right away. You do not have to wait for them to manifest, because you see that the orange blossoms contain the oranges.

The same goes for you. If you are not yet old enough to be a mother, you nevertheless have your children and grandchildren in you. These children and grandchildren are just waiting for their moment to manifest. You contain them all—your father, your mother, and your children. You carry in you the whole of the cosmos. Modern scientists are also beginning to speak this language. They say that one electron is made up of all other electrons, and that an electron may be both here and there at the same time. The language of science is starting to resemble the language of Buddhism.

There is a specific term for the nature that is the true basis of everything. That term is *nirvana*, which means extinction. Nirvana is the extinction of all concepts, and the extinction of the pain that concepts cause. The idea of birth and the idea of death can make you suffer a lot. We find the idea of nonbeing terrifying, so please jut get rid of this concept. You aren't afraid of the kaleidoscope—you don't cry every time an appearance in the kaleidoscope disappears. The same thing is true of life. You don't need to be afraid, because there is neither birth nor death, only successive manifestations. The earth, our mother, has given birth to us thousands and thousands of times. We manifest and then we return to the elements that compose us, only to manifest once again. Nothing is lost. This insight has the ability to get us out of our prison.

Let us come back to the flower. The flower is full of all the elements of the cosmos. It has everything in it, and it is devoid of only one thing: separate existence. Actually, separate existence is something we should not wish for. Isolation is suffering, like being the object of discrimination. A separate existence is something I would never want.

"Interbeing" is a much better verb to use than "being,"

because I am in you and you are in me. This is the teaching of the Christian Gospels as well. The Father is in the Son, the Son is in you, and you are in the Son. You are in the Father, I am in you, and you are in me. That is interbeing.

We can attain this insight through the practice of deep looking. Using the keys of impermanence and non-self, we open the door of reality. This is the work of the meditator. Opening the door of reality and looking at it brings us a great joy because our fear and suffering evaporate. That is worth the effort, isn't it?

How do you use your time? You have to make a living, certainly, and you have to support your loved ones. But do you make the effort to arrange your life so you can do some deep looking? That will bring you joy, freedom from fear, and great well-being. You must not let yourself drown in an ocean of fear and suffering.

There are among us people who have practiced deep looking and shared their insight with us. Take advantage of that. Walk on the spiritual path that lets you touch the depths of your being so that you can free yourself from fear, worries, and despair.

I have my own version of a famous phrase of Shakespeare's: "To be or not to be—that is *not* the question." The real question is whether you can touch the nature of no-birth and no-death. There exist many pairs of conceptual opposites, such as being and nonbeing, birth and death, arriving and departing, one and all. We should get rid of these pairs of opposites. Doing that is realizing the Middle Way, which is what Buddhism teaches. The Middle Way means going beyond all these pairs of opposites.

It's important to understand, though, that after using the keys of impermanence and non-self to open the door of reality, we don't need the keys anymore. If you have used the key of impermanence intelligently to open the door of reality, you do not need that key anymore. The key is not your goal, nor is it an idol to be worshiped.

The Dharma gives you tools, but please do not cling to the Dharma. Liberate yourself from it! You were provided with a raft to cross the river of suffering, but you should not worship it. It is necessary to use the raft with a great deal of intelligence to get to the other side, but once you've arrived there, you don't need it anymore. You shouldn't put the raft on your back and carry it around with you on land.

The teachings of impermanence and non-self are tools you need to work with, but you should not get caught in them. If you do, impermanence becomes just another concept, and so does non-self. These kinds of concepts are exactly what the Buddha said we should get rid of. He said that nirvana is the complete extinction of concepts, including the concepts of impermanence and non-self.

When you want to start a fire, you light a match, and then the fire consumes the match. The teachings of impermanence and non-self are like the match. If you practice with intelligence and succeed in your practice, the match will be consumed and you will be completely free. You will not have to defend Buddhism; you will not have to die for Buddhism. Buddhism has no need for martyrs.

The Dharma is offered to you as a tool, not as an object of worship. Cutting the roots of evil, hate, confusion, and discrimination is the work of all those who meditate, and the Dharma is the sickle we use to do that. If somebody gives you a sickle to cut the grass with, you use it. You don't put it on a shrine or in a special box.

We must also go beyond the concept of nirvana. The word "nirvana" is like the word "God"—it can become a concept for you to get caught in. We should touch God as an ultimate reality and not as a concept. The same thing is true of nirvana. We should touch it as an ultimate reality in the here and now. If nirvana is a concept to you, then you are a prisoner. Burn nirvana, burn impermanence, and burn non-self if they ever become concepts!

SEVEN

Becoming Truly Alive

What would you do if your doctor told you that you only had three months to live? Would you waste this time bemoaning your fate? Would you give yourself over to pain and despair? Or would you resolve to live each moment of those three months in a deep way? If you do that, three months of life is a lot.

Some twenty years ago, a young man came to me and told me exactly this—that he had only three months to live. I asked him to sit down with me and have a cup of tea. "My friend," I said to him, "you must drink this tea in such a way that life is possible. We must live this moment we have together in a deep way."

One day is a lot. A picnic lasts only half a day, but you can live it fully, with a lot of happiness. So why not three months? Your life is a kind of picnic, and you should arrange it intelligently.

Someone I knew once said to his Buddhist teacher, "Master, I would like to go on a picnic with you." The teacher was very busy, so he replied, "Sure, sure, we'll go on a picnic one of these days." Time went by, and five years later they still hadn't had the picnic.

One day the master and the disciple were on some business together, and they found themselves caught in a traffic jam. There were so many people in the street that the master asked the disciple, "What are all these people doing?" The disciple saw that it was a funeral procession. He turned to the master and said, "They're having a picnic."

Don't wait to start living. Live now! Your life should be real in this very moment. If you live like that, three months is a lot! You can live every moment of every day deeply, in touch with the wonders of life. Then you will learn to live, and, at the same time, learn to die. A person who does not know how to die does not know how to live, and vice versa. You should learn to die—to die immediately. This is a practice.

Are you ready to die now? Are you ready to arrange your schedule in such a way that you could die in peace tonight? That may be a challenge, but that's the practice. If you don't do this, you will always be tormented by regret. If you don't want to suffer, if you don't want to be tormented by regret, the only solution is to live every minute you are given in a deep way. That's all there is to it. The only way to deal with insecurity, fear, and suffering is to live the present moment in a profound way. If you do that, you will have no regrets.

That's what the young man who was told he had three months to live chose to do. He decided to live every moment of his life in a very deep way. When he started doing that, he felt the sources of his despair leaving him, and he got himself back on his feet. It was a miracle. Though his doctor had pronounced a kind of death sentence on him, he lived another fifteen years. I gave him the Dharma name *Chân Sinh*, which means "true life." Before he was told he was going to die, he didn't know what real life was. But after that happened, he learned what real life was, because he was there for every moment of every day.

Albert Camus, in his novel *The Stranger*, used the term "the moment of awareness." When the protagonist of the novel, Meursault, learns he is going to be executed for the murder he has committed, anxiety, fear, and anger are born in him. In despair, he is lying on his prison bed looking at the ceiling when, for the first time, he sees the square of blue sky through the skylight. The sky is so blue—it's the first time in his life that he has gotten deeply in touch with the blue sky. He has already lived for decades without ever really seeing the blue sky. Perhaps he has looked at the sky from time to time, but he has not seen it in a deep way. Now, three days before his death, he is able to touch the blue sky in a very deep way. The moment of awareness has manifested.

Meursault decides to live every minute he has left fully and deeply. Here is a prisoner who is practicing deep meditation. He lives his three last days in his cell within that square of blue sky. That is his freedom. On the afternoon of the last day, a Catholic priest comes to Meursault's prison cell to give him the last rites, but Meursault refuses. He doesn't want to waste the few hours left to him talking to the priest, and he doesn't let him come in. He says, "The priest is living like a dead man. He is not living like me, I am truly alive."

Maybe we too are living like dead people. We move about life in our own corpse because we are not touching life in depth. We live a kind of artificial life, with lots of plans, lots of worries and anger. Never are we able to establish ourselves in the here and now and live our lives deeply. We have to wake up! We have to make it possible for the moment of awareness to manifest. This is the practice that will save us—this is the revolution.

Has the most wonderful moment of your life already happened? Ask yourself that question. Most of us will answer that it hasn't happened yet, but that it could happen at any time. No matter how old we are, we tend to feel that the most wonderful moment of our life has not happened yet. We fear maybe it's too late, but we are still hoping. But the truth is, if we continue to live in forgetfulness—that is, without the presence of mindfulness—that moment is never going to happen.

The teaching of the Buddha tells you clearly and plainly to make this the most magnificent and wonderful moment of your life. This present moment must become the most wonderful moment in your life. All you need to transform this present moment into a wonderful one is freedom. All you need to do is free yourself from your worries and preoccupations about the past, the future, and so on.

The deep insight of impermanence is what helps us do this. It is very useful to keep our concentration on impermanence alive. You think the other person in your life is going to be there forever, but that is not true. That person is impermanent, just like you. So if you can do something to make that person happy, you should do it right away. Anything you can do or say to make him or her happy—say it or do it now. It's now or never.

In the practice of Buddhism, dying is very important. It's as important as living. Death is as important as being born, because birth and death inter-are. Without birth, there could be no death. Without death, there is no birth. Birth and death are very close friends, and collaboration between the two of them is necessary for life to be possible.

So do not be afraid of death. Death is just a continuation, and so is birth. At every moment, death is happening in your body—some cells are dying so other cells can come to life. Death is indispensable to life. If there is no death, there is no birth, just as there can be no left if there is no right. Don't hold out hope that life will be possible without death. You must accept both of them—birth and death.

If you practice well, you can gain deep insight into the ultimate dimension while remaining in touch with the historical, or relative, dimension. And when you are deeply in touch with the historical dimension, you also touch the ultimate dimension, and you see that your true nature is no-birth and no-death.

Living is a joy. Dying in order to begin again is also a joy. Starting over is a wonderful thing, and we are starting over constantly. Beginning anew is one of our main practices at Plum Village, and we must die every day in order to renew ourselves, in order to make a fresh start. Learning to die is a very profound practice.

Shariputra's Guidance

Sudatta was a very wealthy businessman in the ancient Indian city of Shravasti and a famous lay disciple of the Buddha's. He had used a great part of his wealth to help the poor, helpless, and orphaned, and so the people of Shravasti gave him the name *Anathapindika*, meaning "supporter of orphans and the helpless," and that is the name we know him by today.

Anathapindika was very devoted to the Buddha. He

spent a lot of money buying a park in Shravasti called the Jeta Grove to turn it into a monastery for the Buddha and a headquarters for the work of the Dharma. In his life he got a great deal of pleasure out of supporting the Buddha, the Dharma, and the Sangha. It was always his joy to support the Three Jewels.

When Anathapindika was nearing death, the Buddha paid him a visit. It had been about thirty years since their first meeting. Over this period, the Buddha had assigned his great disciple Shariputra to take care of Anathapindika and travel with him, so Anathapindika and Shariputra had become very close friends. Now, the Buddha assigned Shariputra to help Anathapindika die in a happy and peaceful way.

Learning that Anathapindika was very close to death, Shariputra asked his young brother in the Dharma, Ananda, a cousin of the Buddha, to accompany him on his alms round, and they stopped at Anathapindika's house. Seeing the two venerable monks, Anathapindika tried to get out of bed, but he was unable to do so. Shariputra said to him, "My friend, lie down. We will get some chairs and come sit with you." After they sat down, Shariputra asked, "My friend Anathapindika, how do you feel in your body? Are your physical pains decreasing or increasing?"

When you are about to die, you have pain in your body, and perhaps in your mind as well—feelings of anxiety, isolation, and confusion. At this moment, which is a very important one in your life, you need help. You need someone with you at this difficult time.

Anathapindika answered Shariputra, "Venerable one, the pains in my body do not seem to be subsiding. They keep increasing. I am suffering more and more."

Then Venerable Shariputra told Anathapindika that the time had come for him to meditate on the Three Jewels. He asked Ananda and Anathapindika to breathe deeply and concentrate on the Buddha, the Dharma, and the Sangha. Then Shariputra conducted a guided meditation.

"The Buddha has attained reality, just as it is," Shariputra said. "The Buddha is completely and truly awakened. He has brought understanding and action to the level of perfection. He has attained genuine happiness. He understands the nature of the world and of men. He is unequaled in wisdom. He is a great man. He is the teacher of both men and gods."

Shariputra said these words to help Anathapindika see clearly who the Buddha really was—a person with a lot of tenderness, compassion, and happiness, someone who was an enormous help to other beings.

Shariputra was one of the Buddha's most intelligent disciples, and he knew precisely what state Anathapindika was in. Shariputra recognized the seeds of happiness in Anathapindika's consciousness, and he knew that Anathapindika took great pleasure in serving the Three Jewels. So to help restore Anathapindika's equanimity, he watered the positive seeds of happiness by inviting him to concentrate on the Buddha, the Dharma, and the Sangha. The practice was very effective. In a few minutes, Anathapindika's pain was considerably reduced and he was able to smile again.

This is a wonderful practice, and we can all learn to do it. A person who is about to die has seeds of suffering in her, but she also has seeds of happiness. You who love this person should recognize the seeds of happiness and suffering in her, and speak to her about the things that evoke happiness in her. It is very important to do this. Even if the person is in a coma, you should speak to her like this. Communication is possible. She will hear you.

I remember going with Sister Chan Khong to visit my friend Alfred Hessler, who was dying in a Catholic hospital in New York State. Alfred was a peace activist who had been a tremendous help to us during the Vietnam War in our efforts to stop the bombing. We worked shoulder to shoulder with him, and we became very close friends.

That day, Sister Chan Khong and I were on our way to a retreat in upstate New York at which six hundred people were expected, and by chance the clinic was on our way. When we entered his room, his daughter, Laura, tried to get Alfred to come out of the coma. "Alfred! Alfred!" she cried out, "Thay is here, Thay is here! Sister Chan Khong is here! Come back!" But Alfred remained in the coma.

Sister Chan Khong then began to sing a verse that is

drawn directly from a sutra written by the Buddha. The words go like this:

> This body is not me, I am not caught in this body.
> I am life without boundaries. I have never been born,
> and I shall never die.
> Look at the ocean and the sky filled with stars,
> manifestations of my wondrous true mind.
> Since before time, I have been free.
> Birth and death are only doors through which we
> pass, sacred thresholds on our journey.
> Birth and death are just a game of hide and seek.
> So laugh with me,
> hold my hand,
> let us say goodbye,
> say goodbye, to meet again soon.
> We meet today.
> We will meet again tomorrow.
> We will meet at the source at every moment.
> We meet each other in all forms of life.

The third time Sister Chan Khong repeated this chant, Alfred came to and opened his eyes. We were very happy. Laura asked him, "Do you know that Thay and Sister Chan Khong are here?" Alfred was unable to speak, but he answered with his eyes that he knew his friends were there.

Then Sister Chan Khong began the practice of watering the seeds of happiness in him. She spoke about our work for peace in Vietnam and, like Anathapindika, how much Alfred had found happiness in this work. "Do you remember the time we were in Rome?" she asked him. "There were three hundred Catholic priests, and each of them carried the name of a Buddhist monk who was imprisoned in Vietnam because he had refused to join the army.

"Alfred, do you remember the time you were in Saigon with the Venerable Tri Quang, the head of the pacifist movement in Vietnam? The night before, the United States had decided to bomb the country. Venerable Tri Quang was furious and refused to see anybody who was American. But you sat down at his door and said that you were a friend and not an enemy. You said, 'I am here to help you, and I am going to stay on a hunger strike until you open your door.' The venerable monk invited you in. Do you remember that?"

Sister Chan Khong practiced watering the positive seeds in him because she knew that Alfred had a great deal of suffering in him. Suddenly, he opened his mouth and said, "Wonderful, wonderful." He repeated it twice. What was wonderful, too, was that at that moment he had friends to help and support him. When it was time for us to go, I said to his family, "Continue the practice. You should talk to him about these things that have brought him happiness."

Another time, Sister Chan Khong's older sister was in a coma and nearing death. She had suffered a great deal.

She lay in bed writhing and moaning and crying out in pain. The doctors did all they could to alleviate her pain, including giving her painkillers, but they were unable to help. Sister Chan Khong arrived with a tape player containing a Vietnamese chant to the bodhisattva of great compassion, chanted by the monks and nuns in Plum Village. She put the headphones over her big sister's ears and turned up the volume so the sound could reach through the coma. Within two minutes her sister stopped writhing and crying out. She became completely peaceful. Why? Because she had in her the seeds of that chant. When she was a little girl, she had gone to the monastery and heard the monks chanting. The seeds of peace, faith, and compassion were in her already. During her life of hard work, she never had taken the time to water these seeds. But as she was dying, Sister Chan Khong was able to help her water them. She became very calm and remained peaceful until her death. The doctors there, including her own daughter who is a doctor, were astonished. None of the drugs had worked. Only that tape was able to break through and allow the seeds of spirituality in this person to be touched. We all have these seeds in us; and it's never too late to touch them.

You Are More Than This Body and Mind

After Shariputra watered the seeds of happiness in Anathapindika by talking about the Three Jewels, he did a guided meditation for him on the six senses.

"Listen, my friend," Shariputra said, "let us practice together. Breathing in, I know that my body is not me. Breathing out, I know I am not caught in this body. These eyes are not me. I am not caught in these eyes. These ears are not me. I am not caught in these ears. This nose is not me. I am not caught in this nose. This tongue is not me. I am not caught in this tongue. This body is not me. I am not caught in this body. This mind is not me. I am not caught in this mind."

We are in the habit of identifying ourselves with our bodies. The idea that we are this body is deeply entrenched in us. But we are not just this body; we are much more than that. The idea that "This body is me and I am this body" is an idea we must get rid of. If we do not, we will suffer a great deal. We are *life*, and life is far vaster than this body, this concept, this mind.

"These mental formations are me"—this is another idea we have to get rid of. Therefore, when someone is dying, above all we have to help them stop identifying with their body and mind. We are not prisoners of our senses. We are not prisoners of our bodies or our minds. We must become free of our body and free of our mind. We must be free of the idea that "I am this body, I am this mind." When we get rid of these ideas, we become greater, deeper, and freer than our mind.

The disintegration of the body is not the end. It is only the cessation of a manifestation. When conditions are no longer sufficient, the manifestation ceases. To light a fire, you need fuel, and as soon as there is no more fuel, the fire goes out. The same is true of the body and mind. Conditions must be sufficient for the manifestation to continue. If not, it will cease and then manifest again sometime in the future.

"These forms are not me, and I am not caught in these forms," Shariputra continued. "These forms are merely objects of sight—when light strikes the eyes, sight manifests as the consciousness of perceiving shapes and colors. I am not those forms.

"When the tongue comes in contact with things that have taste, the consciousness of taste manifests and we perceive flavors. Tastes are not me. I am not caught in tastes. Smells are not me. I am not caught in smells. Tangible objects are not me. I am not caught in these. Thoughts and ideas are not me. I am not caught in thoughts and ideas."

This practice is indispensable for liberation. We must not identify with the sense organs or the sense objects. We must not identify with the six sense consciousnesses—sight, sound, smell, taste, touch, and mind consciousness. These consciousnesses manifest when the necessary conditions come together, and they cease to manifest when the necessary conditions cease to be present. This is something that can be tested and confirmed. It is altogether scientific.

Here is a meditation on the six elements. "Breathing

in, I am aware of the element of earth in me. Breathing out, I recognize it outside and around me. I smile at the earth element in and around me, everywhere. I recognize the element of fire in my body, and I recognize the element of fire in the world around me. I recognize the elements of water, air, space, and consciousness."

These elements inter-are. Each element contains the five other elements. One thing contains all things. Look deeply into the water element, the earth element, heat, air, space, and consciousness; and you will find that each one contains the five others. That is the interbeing nature of the elements.

Shariputra said to Anathapindika, "My friend, things appear and disappear according to causes and conditions. The true nature of things is not being born, and not dying. Birth and death are nothing more than concepts. Our true nature is the nature of no-birth and no-death, and we must touch our true nature in order to be free."

Shariputra continued, "When the body or the mind manifests, we say that it exists, but that is not correct. When a thing has not yet manifested, we say that it does not exist, but that is not correct either. The ideas of being and nonbeing have to be rejected. These notions do not apply to reality. When the conditions come together, your body or your mind manifests.

"Let us look deeply into the five *skandhas:* forms, feelings, perceptions, mental formations, consciousness. There is nothing there that could be called a self. As a result of ignorance, we are caught up in ideas and concepts. But in truth we are free from these ideas and concepts. The true nature of reality is interbeing. The reality of interbeing has the nature of emptiness and of non-self. We are free in the past, and we are free in the present."

At this point in the meditation, Anathapindika began to cry. It was the first time he had touched the profound teachings on emptiness, non-self, interbeing, and so on. He needed this teaching on the nature of no-birth and no-death in order not to suffer, but he had never had the opportunity to practice or study it.

Surprised by Anathapindika's tears, Venerable Ananda asked him, "My friend, why are you crying? Is there something that you regret?"

Anathapindika smiled and replied, "No, Venerable Ananda, I have no regrets. I am crying because I have served the Buddha and the Sangha for so many years, and I have never heard a teaching as profound as the one I have heard today. It is wonderful. I am free."

Venerable Ananda said, "My friend, you don't know it, but this kind of teaching is given every day to the monks and nuns."

"Venerable one," Anathapindika replied, "please tell the Buddha that it is true many laypeople are too busy to learn this teaching and practice. But tell him there are other laypeople who are very capable of receiving this teaching and applying it in their lives. I beg you, go back to the Buddha and convey to him my request to teach this insight to laypeople."

The Venerable Ananda agreed, and the two venerable monks withdrew. The layman Anathapindika died shortly thereafter in a very peaceful manner. This story is told in a discourse entitled "Teachings To Be Given to the Sick." You should study such texts if you wish to attend dying people.

To help dying people, you must be very solid. You must have fearlessness within you. You must be able to touch no-birth and no-death yourself in order to support a person whose manifestation is about to cease. If you want to attend the dying, you must practice. Through practice you can develop the solidity, the fearlessness, and the techniques that make it possible for you to help people to die in peace. We should never forget that dying is as important as living.

Epilogue

Dear friends who are reading this book, perhaps this is the first time you have studied the practice of Dharma. Some positive seeds have been planted in you, and some of the positive seeds already within you have been watered. I encourage you to find a practice community, a Sangha, near you. (A list of practice centers is included at the end of this book; you can also find a more comprehensive worldwide directory of Plum Village Sanghas at www.iamhome.org.) The Sangha is your refuge, your protection, and without it you might not continue to practice and nurture the happiness and peace within you.

Have confidence that you can continue the work of the Buddha and water the seeds of enlightenment and understanding. You can become a torch shining out enlightenment and compassion, not just on those who are near to you, but on the whole society in which you live.

THE FIVE MINDFULNESS TRAININGS

The Five Mindfulness Trainings were developed during the time of the Buddha to be the foundation of practice for the entire practice community, including monastic and lay members. The basis for the trainings is mindfulness. The Five Mindfulness Trainings protect our freedom and make life beautiful. As guidelines for our daily lives, they are the basis of happiness for individuals, couples, families, and society.

The First Training

Aware of the suffering caused by the destruction of life, I vow to cultivate compassion and learn ways to protect the lives of people, animals, plants, and minerals. I am determined not to kill, not to let others kill, and not to condone any act of killing in the world, in my thinking or in my way of life.

The Second Training

Aware of the suffering caused by exploitation, social injustice, stealing, and oppression, I vow to cultivate loving kindness and learn ways to work for the well-being of people, animals, plants, and minerals. I vow to practice generosity by sharing my time, energy, and material resources with those in real need. I am determined not to steal and not to possess anything that should belong to others. I will respect the property of others, but I will prevent others from profiting from human suffering or the suffering of other species on earth.

The Third Training

Aware of the suffering caused by sexual misconduct, I vow to cultivate responsibility and learn ways to protect the safety and integrity of individuals, couples, families, and society. I am determined not to engage in sexual relations without love and a long-term commitment. To preserve the happiness of myself and others, I am determined to respect my commitments and the commitments of others. I will do everything in my power to protect children from sexual abuse and to prevent couples and families from being broken by sexual misconduct.

The Fourth Training

Aware of the suffering caused by unmindful speech and the inability to listen to others, I vow to cultivate loving speech and deep listening in order to bring joy and happiness to others and to relieve others of suffering. Knowing that words can create happiness or suffering, I vow to learn to speak truthfully, with words that inspire self-confidence, joy, and hope. I am determined not to spread news that I do not know to be certain and not to criticize or condemn things of which I am not sure. I will refrain from uttering words that can cause division or discord, or words that can cause the family or the community to break. I will make all efforts to reconcile and resolve all conflicts, however small.

The Fifth Training

Aware of the suffering caused by unmindful consumption, I vow to cultivate good health, both physical and mental, for myself, my family, and my society by practicing mindful eating, drinking, and consuming. I vow to ingest only items that preserve peace, well-being, and joy in my body, in my consciousness, and in the collective body and consciousness of my family and society. I am determined not to use alcohol or any other intoxicant or to ingest foods or other items that contain toxins, such as certain TV programs, magazines, books, films, and conversations. I am aware that to damage my body and my consciousness with these poisons is to betray my ancestors, my parents, my society, and future generations. I will work to transform violence, fear, anger, and confusion in myself and in society by practicing a diet for myself and for society. I understand that a proper diet is crucial for self-transformation and the transformation of society.

PRACTICE CENTERS

United States

Blue Cliff Monastery
Pine Bush, New York
(845) 733-4959
www.bluecliffmonastery.org

Deer Park Monastery
Escondido, California
(760) 291-1003
www.deerparkmonastery.org

France (Dordogne)

Plum Village, Upper Hamlet
(for men and couples)
(33) 5-53-58-48-58
www.plumvillage.org

New Hamlet
(for women and couples)
(33) 5-56-61-66-88
www.plumvillage.org

Lower Hamlet
(for women and couples)
(33) 5-53-94-75-40
www.plumvillage.org

Son Ha Temple
(33) 5-53-22-88-89
www.plumvillage.org

Maison de l'Inspir (near Paris)
(33) 09-51-35-46-34
maisondelinspir@yahoo.fr

Germany

The European Institute of Applied Buddhism
(49) 2291-90-71-373
www.eiab.eu

ABOUT THE AUTHOR

Thich Nhat Hanh (pronounced "tick not hon") is a world-renowned Zen monk, poet, and peace activist who has been nominated for the Nobel Peace Prize. Born in Vietnam, for the past thirty years he has lived in exile in France, where he founded the monastic community of Plum Village. He has also established monastic communities in New York and California. Thich Nhat Hanh travels actively throughout the world, teaching "the art of mindful living" to people of all backgrounds. He is the author of numerous books, including the best-selling *The Miracle of Mindfulness, Peace Is Every Step, True Love,* and *Living Buddha, Living Christ.*

ALSO BY THICH NHAT HANH

from Shambhala Publications

TRUE LOVE

A Practice for Awakening the Heart

In this little treasure, Thich Nhat Hanh offers timeless insight into the nature of real love. With simplicity, warmth, and directness, he explores the four key aspects of love as described in the Buddhist tradition: lovingkindness, compassion, joy, and freedom—explaining how to experience them in our day-to-day lives. Also available as an audiobook.

LIBRARY OF CONGRESS CATALOGING-IN-PUBLICATION DATA

Nhât Hành, Thích.
[Toucher la vie. English]
You are here: discovering the magic of the present moment /
Thich Nhat Hanh; translated from the French by
Sherab Chödzin Kohn; edited by Melvin McLeod.—1st ed.
p. cm.
ISBN 978-1-59030-675-8 (hardcover: alk. paper)
1. Anapanasmrti. 2. Awareness—Religious aspects—Buddhism.
I. McLeod, Melvin. II. Title.
BQ5630.A6N5313 2009
294.3'444—dc22
2009003939